My Life...Welcome to It

LIVING WITH BI-POLAR DISORDER
(ALSO KNOWN AS MANIC DEPRESSION)

Ivy Berry

authorHOUSE®

AuthorHouse™
1663 Liberty Drive, Suite 200
Bloomington, IN 47403
www.authorhouse.com
Phone: 1-800-839-8640

First published by AuthorHouse 8/4/2008

ISBN: 978-1-4389-0654-6 (sc)

Printed in the United States of America
Bloomington, Indiana

This book is printed on acid-free paper.

Dedications

My book is dedicated to Ian, Holz & Becca
for always being there for me.

For understanding me.

For forgiving me.

And especially for loving me through it all.

A Special Thank You To Dr. R. Lee For Saving My Life

DISCLAIMER : My story is true. I have
changed the names of most of the people
involved.

Contents

Chapter 1

A Glimpse Into My Life Growing Up

I was born on Sunday, March 13, 1960. I am the 10th of 12 children so I wasn't too surprised when I was told I was born at home.

My Father was the Midwife. We had a coal-burning furnace at that time so Dad threw the placenta into the furnace. Now I do not remember any of this (obviously) so I will have to go by what I was told. The first, second, 11th and 12th child were born in hospitals but I don't know how many others were. I'm sure I was not the only child born at home.

I only remember bits and pieces of my life between the ages of one and four. I do remember when I went for a nap one of my brother's would play with my hair before I fell asleep. I liked when he played with my hair. (I still like having my hair played with). However, every time I woke up from my naps my hair would have bunches of knots in my hair. I mean actual knots. He would take my hair and put knots in it all over my head.

When I was two years old, my oldest sister had gotten married. She and her new husband were going to Winnipeg to see his parents. Since my sister had never been away from home before she wanted to take something from home with her. She took me. She also toilet trained me while on vacation.

As I grew up my siblings and I were quite vicious to each other at times. Once when I was making toast, my sister went to take it so I went to stab her in the hand with a fork but she moved her hand in time not to be hurt.

I was brought up in a time when washing the floor meant getting down on her hand and knees with a pail of soapy water. We had to wash the floor by scrubbing. My Mom went out and bought a mop and when my youngest sister went to use the mop to wash the floors with, I got extremely angry. It wasn't fair that we had to get down on our hands and knees but she could us a mop. No way! I took that mop and whacked her over the head with it because I was angry that she was able to wash the floor the easy way.

Again, with my youngest sister, I got angry at her one day because she had used my brush. I took it off her and again whacked her in the head with the hard bristle side.

I can't remember what the incident was about but one of my sister's was in the kitchen with one of my brother's and he made my sister mad. She was at one end of the kitchen and he was at the other end when she threw a bread knife at him. Well, he did get hit, but luckily the blade fell off behind her and he was only hit with the handle of the knife.

My sister (just younger than me) and my brother (just older than me) and I used to tease your youngest sister. Her birth was a difficult one, as a result she was slightly bowlegged, and her rear stuck out a bit because of her spine. We used to imitate the way she walked and would say "only deformed people walk like this".

Come to think about it, she got picked on a lot. I think it was partially because my Mom pampered her. I don't think I was the only one who thought this. I know that was the reason for me picking on her.

While the rest of us had to do our own laundry by the age of 14, my Mom was still doing her laundry well into her teens. We used to have tea and toast before going to bed. My Mom always made it for my sister. We had to make our own. As we got older I used to wear her tops and she hated it because I would stretch her tops. I did that intentionally. Sometimes I used to wear her jeans as well. She and I are the tallest girls in the family so her jeans were not too short on me.

I remember once when I was 8 years old one of my brothers and I were climbing on the bedroom furniture. We would jump on the bed, climb up on a large wardrobe, jump down onto a dresser, then jump down to the floor and do it all over again. My foot slipped when I was trying to climb onto the wardrobe. It fell over on top of me. My brother went downstairs to get my Dad to take it off of me. Well I guess this was a sight that everyone in the house had to see. I remember my Mom looking at me and saying "that's what you get for climbing on the furniture". I remember screaming in my head at her. I was really mad when I finally said "is someone going to get this thing off of me". My

Dad lifted it off me and put it back place. Not one person, especially my Parents, asked if I was OK. Not one person checked to see if I hadn't broken my ribs or check for bruising. They didn't know if I was bleeding internally or not. The wardrobe was lifted off me and everyone went back to what they were doing. I was ignored. No one cared if I was hurt or not. I remember this well because I was furious with everyone. At that point I hated everyone.

It was my responsibility to get my youngest sister to school, bring her home for lunch, take her back to school, and then bring her home after school. She used to either sit on the seat or on the fender.

One day, on the way home for lunch, we saw a boy in her class on the sidewalk ahead of us. We were riding on the road. Suddenly he throws a rock in front of my bike. He had been playing with a puppy but didn't expect the puppy to chase the rock. I hit the puppy right smack into his side. My front wheel stopped and my sister and I flew over the handlebars. The owner of the puppy saw everything so she came running out to check on the puppy. She picked it up and took the boy to his home to let his Mother know what he had just done. In the meantime, my sister and I picked ourselves up off the side of the road. I had chipped my front tooth. I had scratches on my face, arms, legs, as well as having a fat lip. My sister faired better. She was just scratched up on her arms and legs. I picked up the bike and we continued on our way home for lunch.

After lunch my Mom tells me to go back to school but my sister got to stay home. I fought with my Mom over this since I was far more hurt than she was. My

Mom got her way and I went back to school for the afternoon.

Another time a new by-law was passed that no one was allowed to double ride on a bike. Again my sister and I were on our way home as we always did. Just one block away from home she spots a police car. She wanted me to stop so she could get off but she was shaking me so hard that we both fell off the bike into a ditch. I had little pebbles in my knees and my hands were scratched up. My sister had scratches as well. Naturally when we got home my Mom cleaned her up and I had to clean myself up.

One day a girl that lived down the street asked me if I wanted to go to the variety store with her before going back to school for the afternoon. I got on my bike and went with her. When I got home after school my Mom told me that I forgot to take my sister to school. Hell, why couldn't one of my other siblings take her or even my Mom? Why was I the only one in charge of this task?

I had siblings going to the same school and older siblings that had to pass our junior school to get to their middle school. Why couldn't one of them take her?

Now this might seem odd, but we did not associate with each other in school. We didn't even go back and forth to school together most of the time.

At the age of 10 there were bullies living on our street. I was very much an introvert, which made me an easy prey for these people. I never made friends in school but I also didn't make friends with my sibling either. I was made fun of by my older siblings. Usually my brothers and sometimes my Brother-In-Laws. They would make comments about my changing body. This made me feel very self-conscious and I hated it.

I was constantly being told to think before I speak. If a thought sounded funny in my head, it came out as an insult. If a thought seemed rational in my head, it came out as stupid. I never really knew how to communicate with my family. I felt intimidated by them sometimes.

In school, if there was too much noise around me I would yell "shut up". This got me sent to the principal's office on more than one occasion. This started when I was in junior school and continued into High school.

At age 14 my Mom arranged for me to baby-sit two kids over the summer. The boy was 10 and his sister was 5. I didn't want this job but my Mother offered my services anyway. I didn't know how to handle kids. I didn't even want to try to amuse them for a day let alone an entire summer.

It was during this summer when my senses started to develop. I knew things were going to happen before they happened. I would get a thought in my head or touch something and know what was going to happen. One day I was playing hockey in the back part of the driveway with the 10 year old. He was talking to me but my mind suddenly shut him out and the image I got was his sister falling down the cement steps with her stroller. Before I could tell him to hush up I heard his sister crying. I told her brother that his sister just fell down the stairs. He looked at me as if to say, how do you know that. I turned and ran and the boy followed. Sure enough she had fallen down the stairs stroller and all. I took her into the house and cleaned her up. Thankfully she wasn't hurt badly. That night the boy told his sister to listen to everything I tell them to do because I was a witch.

Now how do you deal with an event like that? There was no one I could talk to and no one to help me understand what just happened. I wanted to put all of this in the back of my mind and ignore it. I was afraid. How did I know that was going to happen before it happened? How could I see an image before it happened? I was spooked.

Over the years I have learned a few things about myself. Now when I get a thought or touch something and know what is going to happen, I don't freak out. I have accepted it along with the black dots I see out of the corner of my eyes. I have also accepted the voices I hear. It could be someone talking directly to me or it could be the television or radio I hear.

I am learning to tap into this side of me. The telepathic side of me. I meditate and this calms me inside and out. It also allows me to find a peaceful place in my mind. I have a meadow that I am part of. I see all the colours. I feel the soft grass under my feet. I float on the top of the water in my pool. I look up at the sky and see the little puffs of clouds. I can feel the sun on me as well as the breeze. It is such a calm and peaceful place.

I also have visions of at least two past lives. I have a fear of falling down the stairs and I don't know why I have this fear. In one of my lives I see myself falling down the stairs to my death. I don't know yet if I was pushed or if I committed suicide. The odd thing about my visions is that I am actually watching myself fall to my death. How can I be at the top of the stairs and be dead at the bottom of the stairs at the same time? The answer to this was revealed to me by a Reiki master in September of 2007. Apparently I am reliving my death over and over again. Before my reiki session I had mentioned this vision plus the fact that I feel like I was from a wealthy family. I believe I also had a maid. She asked me how I felt about this maid. I told her I hadn't given it any thought. After my session (she had to wake me up because I fell asleep) she told me that she saw me walking toward Jesus (don't know what that meant). She saw my meadow I had described to her. The final thing she told me blew my mind. She told me that my Mother in this life was my maid in my past life. She told me that it was my Mother that pushed me down the stairs because of jealousy and the fact that I paid no attention to her. She had also told me some things that I haven't told anyone. Now if she was brief about these things I probably wouldn't have believed her but she went into detail what she saw. As she told me things some memories started to come back to me about what I thought of my Mother. Not only was she my maid in a past life, but she was also like a maid to me in this life. Up until a certain point in my life, she had to take care of me, bathe me, feed me, change my diapers, and everything else a Mother does while taking care of children. Maybe this is why we had a strained relationship. Maybe that is why she made me do a lot of the chores. Maybe that is why I was the only child to pay rent. She could have had memories of her own and I reminded her of someone. I will never know because she took a lot of secrets with her to her grave.

Now it is up to me to continue my memories of my past lives. Mom and I could have been linked to more than this life and my most recent past life. She never fulfilled her Karmic duty in this lifetime. I am determined to fulfill mine in this lifetime and if I do my Mom and I will never be in each other's lives again. I do believe in reincarnation. I have to, my memories of a past life is too strong to ignore. I will have to find someone to do past life regression on me. I'm looking forward to knowing who I was before and what my life was like. I also have feelings that I did not have children but I do have feelings of being institutionalized.

The other past life I see is in an old western town. Like a one-horse town. The kind that was built during the gold rush. There are cowboys in this vision. I see three men talking outside of a saloon. I am standing across the road from them. I can actually hear them talking but I can't make out what they are saying. One cowboy looks over at me quickly then goes back to talking to his friends. I am wearing a navy blue velvet dress. It has a high neckline and is floor length. After watching these men for a while, I turn around and walk away.

As I have these visions and feelings of past lives, they don't mean much to me at that particular time. Even as I put everything in writing they still don't mean much to me. It was when I was reading my manuscript that things fell into place. For example, I heard "howdy fellas", I had a vision of my husband standing in our bedroom doorway holding a cowboy hat. Then the vision of me watching the 3 cowboys talking. They may or may not be connected, but I feel they are. I really should have a past life regression done. Wish me luck.

Chapter 2
The School Years; Kindergarten to Grade 5

KINDERGARTEN:

I only have a memory of two events. One was when a neighborhood girl was brought into my class for the afternoon. Because I knew her, they sat her beside me.

The other event was when I was caught peeking under a bathroom stall. I was sent into the corner for that.

Sorry, that's all I remember about Kindergarten.

GRADE ONE:

I remember sitting beside a boy I liked. I dropped my pencil on the floor. When I bent over to pick it up, I farted. I was so embarrassed that I pretended that I couldn't reach my pencil. I felt a tap on my back. I picked up my pencil and the boy said, "you farted". I could have died right there and then.

Another time I put my hand up to ask the teacher if I could go to the bathroom. She said "no". I ended up peeing in my pants. When the teacher found out, she opened her desk drawer and said, "Here Ivy, put these on". Well they looked like the biggest pair of underwear I had ever seen and she held them up in from of the whole class. Yet another embarrassing moment in my life where I could have died right there and then.

One day I kept rubbing my right eye. The teacher would call one student up to the front to dismiss the rows. This day she called on me. I went up to the front and the teacher asked me what was wrong with my eye. I told her it feels itchy. I dismissed the rows then the teacher told me to go home and not to come back in the afternoon. She said I had the measles. The teacher was right.

GRADE TWO:

Unbelievably I have no memory of this grade at all. I can't even remember what my teachers name was.

GRADE THREE:

Our teacher was a haggard old witch. At least that's what she looked like to me. She wasn't a very nice to the students. It was almost as if she had no patience with us or she expected us all to be geniuses. I don't remember much more than that. I was just glad to pass this grade so I didn't have her again.

GRADE FOUR:

I remember one day when we were about to do arts and crafts, the teacher put a huge stack of construction paper on the corner of my desk. She bent over to help another student in front of me. I thought it would be funny if I pretended the stack of paper was a pillow. I let out a big yawn, stretched, and then laid my head on the paper. Well, let me tell you, the teacher did not think that this was amusing at all. The teacher sent me to the back of the classroom. I had to turn my back to the class.

As I heard her explaining that we would be weaving the construction sheets into mats, I thought to myself "that sounds pretty easy". I knew how to weave already. However, when the teacher asked me if I had heard the instructions I replied "no". OOPS, another mistake. This time the teacher sent me out into the hall. Luckily, our class was near a fountain and the girl's bathroom. Whenever a student(s) came out of another classroom I would pretend to have a drink from the fountain or I would go and hide in the bathroom until I thought it was safe to come out. Kids aren't stupid. I was laughed at anyway. I had to stay after school and weave a mat before I could go home.

GRADE FIVE:

I liked a boy in my class. We hung out at his house after school. It didn't take long for me to realize he was a nerd. I too was a nerd but he was worse than I was. I'll call him a geek instead because he was a Momma's boy as well. I stopped going to his house and he stopped talking to me.

One time we had to do a project on food. I picked a cocoanut. I drew a beautiful front cover and I was so proud of myself when I handed in my project. The next day we got them back. The teacher commended me on the nice picture I drew however it was a picture of a pineapple, not a cocoanut. OK another time to die of embarrassment. Why is it when you make a mistake teachers feel they have to share that mistake with the entire class. Why couldn't they just hand it to you with a note beside the mistake?

This was also the year that my teacher asked me is I was left-handed. Puzzled, I answered yes. He told me to tilt my paper more to the right and my letters won't be so slanted. Why-O-Why do people feel the need to correct the lefties writing? Even my next-door neighbors insisted that I write with my right hand. As if being left-handed was a curse or something.

One day we had a substitute teacher. She was trying to explain something to the class but the people around me were being too noisy for my liking. I couldn't control myself; I yelled, "Shut up". The teacher looked at me and said, "Do as you say". The whole class was quiet after that. I have never liked a lot of noise around me. It makes me feel flustered and I become enraged.

Well I passed grade five and was now going to start a new school for grades 6, 7, & 8. During my time in junior school not once did I make a good friend. You know, the kind of friendship that you know will stay with you for life. I just didn't have the knack for making friends. I was too shy and too much of an introvert I guess.

Chapter 3
The School Years; Grades 6 to 8

Grade 6:

As if starting a new school wasn't bad enough, my Mother made me start the first day in a maxi dress. Not too embarrassing. I was already 5ft. 7 1/2 inches and there were no maxi dresses long enough for me. I ended up having to wear a maxi dress that was definitely too short on me. It was even ugly to boot.

By far the worst year I have ever had in school. Besides the fact that I had to wear a maxi dress, this was also the year my body was starting to change. Because I didn't speak too much at home I never got up enough nerve to tell my Mom what was happening to me. I had little buds for boobs but never asked my Mom for a bra. This was not a subject my Mom never talked about nor did she offer me any advice. I know she saw the changes in me. I was starting to be teased at school too. The boys would call me "popcorn" because I didn't wear a bra.

One day I decided to wear my bathing suit top as a bra. One of my older sisters noticed this and mentioned it to my Mom. She said it was about time Ivy got a bra. My Mom never said anything to me. She sent one of my brothers to the store to buy a 32AA bra for me. He actually went and did it. Now this is the point that blows my mind. My Mom knew what bra size I needed but didn't do anything about it until my sister intervened. This was what my Mom was like. If you didn't ask her for help she never offered her opinion. I always wondered why she never took it upon herself to take me to the store for a bra. She could have at least told me what was happening to me.

In this grade I was sent to a speech therapist in our school because my R's sounded like W's. They tried to correct this. I simply felt that it was unnecessary because people still knew what I was saying.

I was also sent to another teacher to have me ready a small book aloud and then tell her the meaning of the book. I never said what I was thinking. On one hand I was glad to get out of class but on the other hand I felt the school must have thought I was a complete idiot. I wasn't slow and I wasn't an idiot, I was just shy. That and the fact that I hated school. I always sat low in my seats so that I wouldn't be noticed and hoped the teachers would pick me to answer any questions.

One day in my music class, three of the "popular" girls decided that the next day every girl in class was going to wear a dress to school. Well of course when they saw me walking to school the next day I was wearing pants. They were so cruel to me. They said things like "no wonder you don't have any friends" and that I was a loser. Nice huh? Kids can be so cruel to each other. They didn't know my home life. They didn't know my situation. I never had a dress to wear even if I wanted to. They just assumed every girl must have at least one dress. God how I hated school.

Grade Seven:

There are only four things that I remember about grade seven.

1) I was great at spelling
2) We went on a class trip for three days.
3) My locker was broken into and my lock was gone.
4) I went to my first school dance.

The class trip we went on was in a conservation area and we were sleeping over for two nights. Of all the people to be put in a room with, I was put in the same room as the three "popular" girls that teased me last year. I couldn't wait for the trip to end.

Funny thing about my locker being broken into. The next day one of the teachers had all of his stuff put in it. I was wondering if he would jump in my grave that fast. I not only had to buy a new lock but they had to find me a new locker instead of giving me my old one back. Mom wasn't too pleased about having to buy a new lock because money was always tight.

I was excited about going to my first school dance. My Mom gave me one of my older sister's dresses to wear. This was a bridesmaid dress and it looked like it was made out of couch material. Not only was it too big for me it was too short too. I had to use safety pins to keep my bra straps from being shown. Well naturally someone noticed the pins and made fun of the way the dress fit me. I ended up spending the rest of the time in the girl's bathroom until one of my brothers picked me up.

GRADE EIGHT:

Sorry, this is another grade where I don't remember much. They still sent me to the reading classes. I felt like yelling at them and say I'm not stupid; I'm just not interested in participating during class.

I do remember the teacher. We would laugh at her because it looked like she wore a whole bottle of liquid foundation and then put her head in the oven to bake it onto her face. She would scold us if we wore make-up and here she was with so much make-up it must cost her a fortune.

Passing grade eight was a huge relief to me. That meant I only had one more school to get through. I really did hope High School was going to be better for me. It was a chance for me to start new and make friends.

Chapter 4
The School Years; Grades 9 to 12

Grade Nine:

Why did I think everything would change in High School? There were new people and a completely new bunch of "popular girls". However, this was the first year I had a steady boyfriend. I will call him "John". We met at a local ice rink. He was already seeing someone and I had no thoughts of having a boyfriend. It surprised me when he asked me to go out with him. He told me he was already seeing someone but that he would break up wither to go out with me. What do boyfriends and girlfriends do together? I have never kissed anyone before. Are we supposed to kiss? I don't mind holding hands but anything further than that I didn't know what to do. Even some of the girls at school couldn't believe that I had a boyfriend. Me? The girl that did not talk much. Me? The girl that did not have friends. Me? Yes, me.

I was at a local sledding hill with some of my siblings when I saw "John" at the swings in the park with the girl he was currently seeing. My heart sunk a little. I then decided that I didn't want to be his girlfriend anyway. I put it out of my mind and continued to have fun with my siblings.

The next day "John" showed up at my school and told me that he was at the park the night before to tell his girlfriend that he was breaking up with her because he had found someone new. I didn't tell him that I saw him there. My heart was happy now.

After about six months of dating him, I got bored. The one thing I could always do was turn off and on my emotions whenever I wanted to. I was turned off him now and I told him so. Besides his family did not approve of me because I was not Catholic. He told me that we would break up when he says it is time to break up.

He told me what I could and could not wear in public. He had his friends follow me around and report to him. Geez, this went on for three years. His family owned a paving company. One day, in the summer, they were doing a driveway across the road from where I lived. A neighbor and I were watching them and making fun of them as well. We then decided to go to the variety store. I asked her to wait while I changed my clothes. I went and put on short shorts and a halter-top. I knew this would make him mad. Sure enough, when he came over the night he gave me shit for what I wore in public. I just laughed.

He went to a Catholic School and one night he took me to a school dance. We sat up in the stands. Suddenly he said he had to go and say Hi to a few people, leaving me sitting alone with a bunch of strangers. Next thing I notice, he is dancing with some girl, then another and another and another. By this time the anger that was building up in me was about to explode. I got up and walked out of the gym. I was going to get my coat and go home. "John" must have noticed that I was gone because he came down the hall calling my name. I just kept walking. When he finally caught up with me he asked me, what was wrong and where did I think I was going. Well I just exploded. Yelling at the top of my lungs, I told him what I really thought of him. Now remember, this was not usual behavior for me. I hardly spoke let alone yell at someone in public. It felt good. Now it was someone else's turn to feel embarrassed. These feelings of anger and rage came quickly to me now. I did not know why, but it did. I started to let people know my feelings. This did not go over too well with some people but I did not care anymore. I have put up with so much in my life up to this point that it was about time I pushed back.

One day, at my home, "John" made me so mad that I literally put him up against the wall with one and scratched his face with the other. I drew blood but I did not care. I told him to leave my house and never come back. I then went upstairs to have a nap. I always felt exhausted after I let me rage out. When I came back downstairs, "John" was sitting at our kitchen table. The anger came rushing back. He had managed to make my family feel sorry for him because of what I had done to his face. I did not feel sorry for him. I told him to get the hell out of my house and I told my family members to mind their own business. Something was definitely changing within me.

I had a job at a bookstore in a local mall and "John" worked in a stationary store in the same mall. We would take the bus home together. Then he would walk me the rest of the way home. One day we were on the bus when he told me he had met someone else. I was so elated but kept this feeling to myself. He could not understand why I was not upset and crying. I had been waiting for this day. The bus driver looked back and gave me a little smile.

On this particular day, my Father met me at the bus stop. "John" started to walk with us when I told him he could go home on his own because I was with my Dad. I told my Dad that we had just broken up. My Dad did not ask any questions or say anything but I knew he was happy. He never liked "John" anyway. "John" ended up marrying this girl and the funny thing is that she is not Catholic either.

This was the year I had my first suicidal thought. I was in the girl's locker room getting changed for gym class. Everyone was already in the gym when I noticed the First aid kit. I opened it and saw a full bottle of aspirin. Instantly I thought that if I take this whole bottle of pills and died nobody would miss me. My family does not even know I exist so why keep living. It was at that moment when another student came into the locker room and told me that the teacher wants me in the gym. The girl saw what I had in my hands and gave me a puzzled look. I just put the bottle back where I got it from and went to class.

What I remember of grade 10 is taking classes that I have carried with me to today. I took typing, media studies, home economics, history, & law.

The reason why I remember these classes is because they were all interesting to me. I had become a very fast typist (no bragging, but I still am today).

In Media Studies, we watched a lot of films or short clips in which we had to pick out the differences between one shot to the next. For example, in one scene, a person's drink may be full but when they re-shot the same scene, the drink was not as full. Little things like that but even today, I pick out the discrepancies between one shot to the next, one scene to the next. We would even pick out differences in commercials as well.

In Home Economics half the year we would be sewing clothes and the other half of the year we would be baking or cooking small meals. We would be in groups of four people and had a riot trying to decipher what the ingredients were that we need for baking a particular food. I had a lot of fun in this class. I even earned an extra ½ credit in the sewing part of the course. We were given a project to do regarding certain clothing worn in a certain time or era. My project was on my Dad during World War II. As a part of my project, I had brought my Dad's Spats that he wore over his boots. It was because I brought in a visual that earned me the extra ½ credit. I was so proud of myself.

In history, the only reason why I remember this class as well as did well in this class was because the male teacher we had was very good looking. He was also very friendly to the students. You could tell he liked his job because unlike some teachers, he was not just a robot going through the course. He was actually interested in us learning about all history.

In law class, I really paid attention. This class fascinated me. I have always been interested in law even before I took a law class. I remember near the end of the year asking my teacher her opinion about me continuing a course in law after graduation. She was not trying to discourage me when she told me that law was still a man's job and that it was harder for women to get into law than it was for a man. Now remember this is in 1974 / 1975 and it was not only law that women had trouble getting into. A lot of the careers (like Doctor's for example) were for the men and the jobs were for the women. Thanks goodness times have changed greatly because we have a lot of good female Doctors and Lawyers.

Oh yes, and in Grade 10 I had to take a Grade 9 & 10 math class because I had failed grade 9 math the previous year. It was not until half way through the school year that I was told I could not take two math classes in the same year. However, since half the year was gone they allowed me to stay both classes. Thank goodness for that. I hated math and I knew that I did not have to take math in grade 11. I really wanted to get math over with.

GRADE ELEVEN:

I continued to take the courses from Grade 10 that I enjoyed (except math). Taking these courses definitely made my high school years easier to bear but I still hated school anyway.

I had another one of my many anger attacks when the classroom got too loud for me. I was in Geography class and we were watching a movie. Some of my classmates didn't care for watching movies so they just talked among themselves. Problem was I was sitting near them and I wanted to hear the movie not their gossip.

I couldn't help myself when I yelled out "Shut Up". That got me sent down to the principal's office yet again.

I remember being in the library one day and I was looking through a book (unfortunately I don't remember the name of the book) and I turned to a page that showed a Cyclopes. This picture frightened me so much I could feel a cold chill come over me. I still remember the picture because it was such a shocking reaction I had to the picture. I don't know why it bothered me but I felt fear the entire day. Very strange that I still remember my reaction to this day.

I tend to remember only the traumatic events in my life and not so much of the nice times. I must have had some good times during my childhood. If only I could remember them.

This was the year that "John" dumped me and I started dating "Chris". I had met him through one of my brothers. They worked together. When "John" discovered I was seeing another guy so shortly after our break up he called me at home. He told me how much he missed me and that he still loved me. With no feelings in my heart for him, I reminded him that he was the one that dumped me. I also told him that I didn't want him calling me anymore.

"Chris" was completely different from "John". He didn't tell me what to wear, where to go, people I could hang around with. What a breath of fresh air. He had dropped by my school one day. A girl with a locker beside mind asked me how much I paid him to go out with me. I asked her why she would say such a thing. She said it was because "John" was not very good looking but that "Chris" was very handsome. She was joking about me paying "Chris" of course. "Chris" and I dated from 1977 to 1982 before we called it quits. "Chris" and I were complete opposites. I liked to party and have fun and he didn't. He was into cars and hung around with his cousin. It was me this time that didn't like his family. They were too prissy for me. Shortly after we broke up, I started dating Robert. I had moved into another apartment that "Chris" and I were to share (until he backed out of the deal). "Chris" came to the door one night while Robert was there. I asked him what he wanted and he just barged in. He went straight for my bedroom where Robert was sleeping. "Chris" hit Robert over the head with a pillow, which got Robert up. Robert was now ready for a fight if that was what "Chris" wanted. Instead, I put "Chris" up against the wall and asked him what the hell he thought he was doing barging in like he did. He told me that he heard Robert had gotten me into taking drugs. I asked him if he was crazy because he knew I didn't do drugs. I held him up against the wall until he calmed down. When I let him go, I escorted him out of my apartment. He said he still loved me. Why is it, when two people break up one of them gets jealous if the other one starts dating right away? I guess "Chris" thought I would be devastated after five years of a relationship. It was a mutual break-up. We both knew we were not going to marry each other.

GRADE TWELVE:

Finally, it was my last year of school. Nothing extraordinary happened this year in school but at least I graduated. I can't even get myself to enroll in any correspondence course because the thought of doing homework stops me from enrolling. I was still seeing "Chris" at this time. Pretty much the only thing I remember about grade 12 was graduating. My Mom had bought me a new outfit and both my Parents were there when I got my diploma. There were a lot of people at the school that night. I found "Chris" out in the hall. I asked him if he had seen my Parents and he said he hadn't. We searched for them but couldn't find them. I thought they had already gone home so "Chris" and I left. When I got home, my Parents were not there. "Chris" and I waited on the porch until they showed up. That's it. I really do not remember much about grade 12, sorry.

NOTE: While writing this book, I became frustrated a few times because I couldn't remember my younger years. I would read my manuscript repeatedly, but still couldn't understand why I can't remember. I don't know if it is because my life was full of constant criticism by family, classmates, bullies, and even sometimes by my teachers, that I have blocked a lot out. It may simply be that my life was so boring that it was not even worth remembering. Either way, I have wracked my brains over it and just simply cannot remember.

CHILDREN LEARN WHAT THEY LIVE

If a child lives with criticism,
He learns to condemn.
If a child lives with hostility,
He learns to fight.
If a child lives with ridicule,
He learns to be shy.
If a child lives with shames,
He learns to feel guilty.
If a child lives with tolerance,
He learns to be patient.
If a child lives with encouragement,
He learns confidence.
If a child lives with praise,
He learns to appreciate.
If a child lives with fairness,
He learns justice.
If a child lives with security,
He learns to have faith.
If a child lives with approval,
He learns to like himself.
If a child lives with acceptance and friendship,
He learns to find live in the world.

Remember this saying and learn from it. I have.

Chapter 5
My Relationship With My Mother

The relationship we had was a love/hate relationship. It was very strained to say the least. All my life we butt heads. We just didn't know how to communicate with each other. She didn't have this relationship with any of her other children.

When I was in grade 9, I had started to save my milk money and allowances. I had managed to save $20.00 (in 1974 that was a lot of money). My youngest sister saw the money I had saved and told my Mom. Instead of allowing me to continue saving money, my Mom told me that I had to take my two youngest sisters to a fair that was going on at a school nearby. She wanted me to spend my money on my sisters. I felt this was unfair but my youngest sister always managed to get her way.

I don't think my Mom disliked me, it felt more as if she resented me for some reason. Maybe I reminded her of someone that she didn't care very much for.

I remember being in the kitchen with my Mom and I was wearing something she didn't like. I told her "if you don't like it, don't look". She whacked me across the mouth. I had one of my many tiffs with my Mother and I told her I didn't love her. Her reply was that she didn't love me either. After this, our relationship became strained more than ever. We would have our good moments too, but they were rare. Sometimes she would be so sentimental and other times she was as tough as nails showing no emotions at all.

I also noticed that my Mom was a completely different person when someone from outside the family was around. She would act as if she had an air about her. She was friendly and talked well of her children. She would joke around, laugh, and definitely be a different person. These are the times she was the Mother I wanted, the Mother I needed. However, she also carried another air about her. I got the feeling that she thought she was owed something. That she was better than her life showed. She would tell us that she was related to the later Lester B. Pearson. She also said that decades ago there was royalty in her family. I think she said there was a Duke on the Pearson side of her family. She would tell us she was a twin and that her Mother couldn't take care of all her children so she let a Doctor's family adopt the twin. Other times she would deny saying this. The older she got the more she couldn't keep her stores straight. When confronted about the discrepancies in her stores, she would change the subject.

There were times when I thought my Mom had no class. The Queen Mum was coming to Toronto inspect her troops, The Toronto Scottish. My Dad was in the Toronto Scottish. I was in my early twenties. I had driven my Mom and Dad to University Avenue in Toronto, Ontario where Queen Mum was going to be. My Dad was in his kilt and my Mom was dressed just as the Queen Mum would dress. The matching hat and dress with long white gloves. While my Dad was lined up for inspection, I stood back on the grass and watched my Mum nudge her way to the rope that had cordoned off the sidewalk the Queen Mum was to walk on. My Mom was about the same size and height as the Queen Mum and while my Mom was in line, she made sure the Queen Mum saw her. She called out "Queen Mum" so that the Queen Mum would look over her way. My Mom wanted to be noticed and acknowledged. She got her wish. The Queen Mum looked over at my Mom and smiled while she waved at her.

I don't know why, but I felt embarrassed and was glad that I was nowhere near her at that time. I made my way closer to my Dad as Queen Mum inspected the troops. I was so proud of my Father, standing so straight and at attention. The Queen Mum was talking to the man standing beside my Father and while most people would sneak a glance at the Queen Mum, my Father just stood at attention, eyes straight ahead. There is actually a picture of this in a newspaper but I can't remember which paper it was. One of my brother's has this picture framed.

Whenever Mom and Dad would go out to functions involving the Legion, the Toronto Scottish, on Parade (they were both flag bearers for the Legion), Weddings, etc. my Mom would look very beautiful all dressed up. She wore simple powder foundation and lipstick. Her hair would be done up nice and she smiled a lot more. If I went to any of these functions with them, I was proud of both my Parents for looking so nice and being well behaved. My Dad always behaved himself, but there were times when my Mom would get a little out of control.

As soon as they got home, my Mom would rush into the house so that she could take out her teeth and get out of her clothes so she could put one of her Muumuus on. Now she just looked like a regular old woman. I don't know why I felt embarrassed at these times. She always looked so nice when she was dressed up. Why couldn't she try to look nice at home too?

One time when a couple of siblings and I were going to the annual Legion picnic without my parents, my Mom yelled out the window "now don't embarrass me". Who did she think she was, asking us not to embarrass her? I always wanted to yell back "don't embarrass us either".

I was quite often embarrassed by her. Not that she would intentionally embarrass me; I was just embarrassed by some of her actions, especially if she had been drinking. She would become argumentative and always thought she was right.

After I had graduated grade 12 I thought I could take the summer off and just sit around before looking for a job. I had no particular trade except for typing. I had no idea what I wanted to do with my life. My Mom however, had different plans for me. She wanted me to get a job right away so that's what I did.

Our relationship was still strained. She was now asking me to pay rent for living under her roof. Years later, I discovered that I was the only child that was asked to pay rent. I think it was her way of getting back at me for some reason. She did not want me around but if I was going to stay, I was going to pay for it.

That winter I found an apartment. If I was going to pay rent, I wanted it to be for my benefit, not hers. This was on a Sunday and I told her I was moving out on Friday. Her response was "OK". That was it, OK. She never asked why. She never told me that she would miss me. She did not even try to talk me out of it. Nothing. She did not even have any emotion on her face. She wanted me gone.

I have a nephew with Tourette syndrome. When my brother found out, he told the rest of us. Suddenly we understood why some of us have twitches. This also helped my brother understand his childhood. He used to be considered a troubled student in school. When he went to bed for the night he had to shake his head back and forth in order to get to sleep.

My Mom refused to believe that there was anything wrong in our family and that we certainly did not inherit anything from her side or my Dads side of the families. One of my older sisters had done some research into our families. She discovered that not only was I bi-polar but that we have cousins, aunts, etc. for generations back that have all had some sort of mental illness of some sort. When I was first diagnosed, I spoke to my family asking if they knew of anyone else in the family with a mental illness. All the answers came up no. I thought this odd because I was sure bi-polar was genetic. I thank my sister for doing her research so I now know I am not the only one.

My Mother grew up with a stern Mother of her own. If there was anything wrong within the family circle, it was never talked about. You also never, ever air your dirty laundry in public. This is why I think my Mother was the way she was. Refusing to admit that there were disorders in our family. I believe that my Mother had a disorder of some sort as well but she would never admit to it.

Chapter 6
My Relationship with my Father

Up until the time I moved out on my own, I didn't think that my Father even knew that I existed. To me he was this tall man with big hands that used to spank me when I was young. I don't recall having even one conversation with him up to the time I moved out.

That quickly changed for me a week after I moved out. I called home to talk to one of my sisters and my Dad answered the phone. I asked to talk to my sister when my Dad asked me when I was coming back home again. He said he missed me. Well let me tell you, when he said that to me a whole flood of emotions came out of me. Someone loved me after all. I was missed. I was wanted.

After that day, I did everything I could just to be with my Dad. I had 18 years to make up for. With him saying he missed me, I realized that I loved him too. The more I did for him the more I got to know the man he was. My love for him grew stronger every day and that strong love I had for him before he passed away still exists in me today. I loved him so much that I would forgive him anything. He never hurt my feelings. He never talked down to me and he certainly didn't make me feel that I was a house cleaner to him. That's how my Mother made me feel, but never my Dad.

Dad and I started to do a lot together. We would go bowling, both five and ten pin. Other siblings and friends would come along as well and the goal was to try and beat Dad at least once in any sport. Not only did we bowl, we played darts, we played pool, we played snooker and just couldn't beat him. Not even in shuffleboard. He was good at everything he did but never gloated. Playing cards with him was fun too. He used to play the guitar as well. Whenever the family got together, we couldn't wait until Dad pulled out his guitar. He taught himself to play and he was good at it. He would sing us song from his generation. We learned some old songs because of him.

He belonged to the Fort York Armories. He was a steward in the Sergeant's Mess. I would drive him to the Armories. I would sometimes work with him behind the bar. It was especially fun on Warrior's Day. The room would be packed and my Dad had a special knack for "making mistake" on drink orders. Watching this was hilarious. I used to drive him to the Armories the day after any event. Boy did that room stink. It still had the smell of booze, cigarettes, and cigars because the room was locked up every night. We would have to open all the windows, even in the winter, just to try and air the place out. We would then wash the floors and clean up the tables. We had to do a count on the beer, alcohol, peanuts, etc.

My brothers and brother-in-laws always took Dad golfing. He was damned good at it too. It was unfortunate that I never got to golf with him. I took up golfing the year after he died. He would go on any golfing event that came up.

My Dad had so many friends it was hard to believe. He not only belonged to the Toronto Scottish but was also a Legion member and would involve himself in any activity going on in either place. He would go on parades. He joined the dart league. He was on a bowling league. He was on a euchre league.

I don't know of anyone who did not like my Father. He was fun to be with and was loved by a lot of people outside of the family too. He was even invited to a stag by one of my brother-in-laws for a person that was getting married at our work.

He was the type of man whose door was always open for anyone who wanted to drop by. He didn't dislike anyone. All of his children loved him deeply. He would come up with some pretty corny jokes too.

In September 1987, I was eight months pregnant with my first child when my father had a massive heart attack. I was going to be staying at my Parents house for a while because my husband and I were not getting along. I saw my Dad walk across the front lawn and into the house. This was not his nature. If he saw you, he would stop and wait for you or at the very least acknowledge you. I know he saw me so I couldn't understand why he didn't wait for me. When I got into the house, he was in the bathroom. I asked my Mom what was going on and she said she didn't know. He was supposed to be going to the Fort York Armories to do their banking. He had taken the bus to the subway and while on the subway, he didn't feel well. He got off the subway and lay on a bench for a few minutes. He then went over to the other platform to take the subway and bus back home again. He was only two stops away from where he was supposed to get off in the first place. He thought it hernia was acting up. I knew different. I asked him if his left arm tingled down to his elbow. He said both his arms tingled to the elbows. I immediately went to call 911 and my Mother tried to stop me. She said, "He's in the bathroom". I told her I didn't care where he was all I cared about was the fact that he was having a heart attack and I was going to call for help.

I dialed 911 and told them my Father was having a heart attack. When the ambulance got to our house, they could not fit the gurney into the house so they asked my Dad to get up and walk to the gurney. I think my Dad told them that his hernia was acting up instead of telling them he was having a heart attack. They put him in the ambulance and left. I asked the police if they could escort me to the hospital. The police were in no hurry to get to the hospital so the drove at a normal speed. Unbelievably, we got to the hospital well before the ambulance did. Once I found out my Dad did have a massive heart attack I felt like attacking the ambulance drivers. They were lucky they got him to the hospital when they did. If he had of died on route I would have sued them. The hospital then started to receive a lot of family members showing up to see how Dad was.

After a while, some of them went back to my Mom's house to wait for the news and some of us stayed at the hospital. My Dad was taken up to ICU. My Mother, two brothers, and I went with him but we had to wait in the hall. Suddenly a nurse comes out and asked, "Which one of you is Mrs. Johnston"? I told her I was. She had a message from my Dad. He wanted to know how I was doing. I couldn't believe it, here he is in ICU after having a massive heart attack, and he was worried about me because I was pregnant. I told the nurse to reassure him that I was doing fine and for him not to worry.

I think he was released a few days later. He was put on nitroglycerine pills in case of further attacks. Well sure enough, when I was visiting him at home he had another attack. I froze. My sister kept yelling at me to put a pill under his tongue. I couldn't move. She ended up doing it instead. It was an angina attack. He ended up back in the hospital and they operated on him. He had a quadruple bypass and the Doctor said, "I just added another ten years to your life". My Dad's reply was "what the hell am I going to do with another ten years"? He was joking of course. He was happy to have another ten years with us.

Ten years is what he had. In April 1997, just a couple of weeks before he would have turned 75, he passed away in his sleep. I still miss him today just as much as I missed him when I found out he died. I have not gotten over his death yet. He died too suddenly for me. I was at work when I was told that the ambulance had been called. I thought that he would end up in the hospital again. I did not want to see him with tubes in him again. It broke my heart to see him like that. I decided to stay at work. An hour later, I got a call at work. It was one of my brother-in-law's and he told me that Dad was dead. I screamed and cried. I could not believe what he was telling me. In my mind, he was supposed to be in the hospital not dead. I could not fathom it. Not my Dad. Oh how my heart ached.

Apparently, he was already dead when I was told the ambulance was called but I wasn't told until it was confirmed.

My heart still aches for him today the same as it did in April 1997. Even today, I still cry for him. My Dad was my hero and hero's do not die. He still lives within me every time I take a breath.

One Christmas I had bought my Father a wedding band because he lost his during WWII. I had it engraved saying with love from Ivy Sr. & Jr. This gift even surprised my Mom. He was a very hard person to buy for because he didn't need anything. I wanted to get him something different. That is when the ring came to mind. Now, I know what you're thinking. I married my Dad. That was definitely not my thought when I bought it for him. I just wanted to get him something different.

When he died, his ring came back to me. I wore it on a chain around my neck. One day my Mom and sister had come over to my house. This was now a few years after my Dad died. I asked my Mom if she would like to borrow his ring for a while. She said yes, so I put it around her neck.

She knew this was only temporary and that I could ask for the ring back at any time. She called me in May 2001 and asked me if I wanted the ring back. I told her I was going in for a minor operation and if I survived, I would have Ian go to her place and pick it up. By this time, she was wearing the ring on her wedding finger and then put her rings on top. He rings were too tight to get off so she had to use soap to take her rings off and put my Dad's ring on, and then her rings on after that.

I was in and out of the hospital in 23 hours. I called her when I got home and told her that Ian was going to pick up the ring. She quite calmly told me she lost them. All of them, including hers. She thinks she lost them planting flowers. The she told me she lost them doing the laundry. If that was me and I lost my rings, I would be turning everything upside down. I would even dig up the flowers I just laid. Not her. To this day, I still have no idea who she gave the rings to. No, she was not buried with them.

I know that when it is time, my Dad will help me get his ring back. Until then, everyone in the family knows I am looking for it. I just have to be patient until then.

Chapter 7
Life on My Own

Shortly after graduating, I got my first job. I moved out of my parent's house in 1978. I got a one-bedroom apartment close to where "Chris" lived but still on the bus route to my job. I started to make friends at work and we would all go to the bars on a Friday after work. Chris was a year older than I was. He had his own car. We would go up to his cottage. We would cruise Yonge Street. I was now enjoying my life. I felt like I was finally coming into my own. I could do whatever I wanted to do. I could stay out late. I had no one to answer to except myself. I was having the time of my life. This was also the year I became self-harming. I was anorexic. I would scratch myself up and draw blood. I would punch myself in the eye until it was too sore to punch anymore. I don't know why I felt the need to hurt myself. I think it was partially for the attention I got but also because I wanted "Chris" to see me more. I was hoping he would think that living on my own I might need him around more to protect me. I think I felt the need to be the center of attention or at the very least, there would be someone who cared enough about me to try to help me. This never happened.

At first, our relationship was based on caring for each other. After the first year it graduated into seeing each other if we were not busy doing something else with other people. I would only go over to his house on the weekends in the summer because his parents went to their cottage then. I was starting to feel unloved again, just like when I was growing up. There was a guy at my work that was interested in me. I'll call him "Phil". He would buy me little gifts or meet me for breakfast. He bought me gifts on my birthday. One day, when I came back from lunch I went straight to my superior's desk to ask her a few questions. About a minute later, the guy that liked me came out from under my desk. All the other girls knew he was hiding there and because I didn't go straight to my desk, I ruined the surprise. Everyone was laughing. It had backfired on him. He would also drive me home some nights and wanted to be invited upstairs but I never would ask him to come up. He knew I had a boyfriend; I never kept that a secret. "Chris" came to pick me up after work one day and I introduced the two of them. "Phil" actually said to "Chris" "I was hoping you were a figment of her imagination". "Phil" ended up getting a job somewhere else and we never stayed in touch.

That was another problem with me. I never stayed in touch with people. If you were in my life and I was hanging around with you for a while, I would keep in touch. However, once you moved away or got another job somewhere else, I would never call you again. I have never been one for talking on the phone for extended periods of time. If you didn't call me first, I wouldn't call you at all.

When I was 21, one of my sisters had moved in with me. Her boyfriend and Chris became good friends. Sometimes all four of us would have dinner together at our apartment. Now this was hilarious. My sister and I could not cook for beans. We never managed to get the timing right. The chicken would be cooked, but the potatoes were still boiling. By the time the potatoes were cooked, the chicken was cold or dried out. We tried broiling steaks one time (and one time only) but they turned out like shoe leather. Needless to say, my sister and I didn't have our guys over for dinner anymore.

I had pushed back all the weird things that had happened when I was 14 and called a witch. I had pushed them so far back in my mind that I forgot about each event, or so I thought.

In one of the other apartment's I had made friends with a guy who did Tarot readings. He would tell me things about myself that nobody else knew. He even knew when my birthday was without me telling him. One time "Chris" and I went to "Jeff's" apartment (not his real name). "Jeff" pulled out his Tarot cards and had me shuffle them, then cut them. I handed the deck back to him. He started to flip over a few of the cards. Then he would sit back and look at them. He told me that my soul mate is tall with dark hair, then turned to "Chris", and said "but it's not you". "Chris" was upset by this and shortly after we left "Jeff's" apartment. I never forgot what "Jeff" said.

About a year went by without any incidents until one night. My sister and I had been out for the night. When we got home, she parked the car in front of the building beside ours instead of using our parking space at the back of our building. As soon as I touched her door handle I told her to move her car it was going to be hit. She didn't feel like moving the car so we got out of the car and went up to our apartment.

We were in our beds asleep when for some reason I woke up. It was about 1:00am and my bed was beside the window. I never wondered why I woke up (not my usual habit) but I decided it was such a nice night I would sit there and look out the window for a while. As I was looking out the window, I see this black car and since there was no other traffic on the street, my eyes went directly to him. Then BANG, he hits my sister's car. By the way, her car was the only car parked on the street that night. I jumped over my bed and woke up my sister to tell her that her car just was hit.

It didn't take long for the residences in the apartment to go outside to see what happened. I went directly to "Jeff" and told him that as soon as I touched her door handle I knew her car was going to be hit. He teased me by humming the tune to The Twilight Zone. However, I knew that he believed me. I then realized why I woke up and looked out the window. I was meant to witness this accident.

My sister and I lived together for about a year. Her boyfriend was going to Western University in London, Ontario. She had decided to go and live in London to be closer to him. I no longer wanted to live on my own so I moved back home again. After a while, this situation started to cramp our style. "Chris" and I were used to coming and going as we pleased. (He had a key to my apartment) I decided to look for another apartment. This time "Chris" said he would move in with me. After signing the contract "Chris" told me he wasn't moving in with me so I had to pay the rent on my own. This was the beginning of the end of our relationship. The sister that used to live with me got an apartment in the same building. I thought at first this would be great because there would be someone I could go visit and she would come and visit me. It didn't quite work out that way. I went to her apartment mostly. I don't think she ever went to my apartment. She was now married and I felt like I was intruding every time I went to her place. As a result we did not hang out a lot with each other. Just like when we were kids, we lived together but never really associated with each other.

Not too long after moving in "Chris" and I broke up. We had picked out an engagement ring but did not know how to tell me he did not want to marry me. He spoke with his Mom about this. When I went over to his place he explained exactly how he felt and that he could not go through with the engagement. To his amazement, I agreed. We were just too opposite and we would probably end up divorced anyway. He was quite surprised by my reaction. He soon realized that I felt the same way he did. We were both relieved. Besides, I was fooling around on my behind his back. I fooled around with his cousin, his best friend, some of my co-workers. I guess I was still looking for someone to love me enough to care deeply for me. He gave me the ring anyway and I gave it to my Dad to give to my Mom for Christmas. I had gone to a friend's New Years Eve party and that was where I met my first husband Robert. He was the DJ at the party.

Chapter 8
The Working Years

My first job was for a financing company in uptown Toronto. They trained me and within two weeks, I had caught on. I became very proficient at what I had to do that they gave me other jobs to do as well just so I could keep busy. I have, and still do not, like to pretend to be busy. It bored me to just sit around and do nothing. Approximately two years later, the company had changed its name and moved to downtown Toronto. Now our workload had increased in the department I worked. This suited me better because now I was constantly busy and the days went by faster. At this stage of my life, I was already living on my own.

This is also around the time that I started self-harming myself. I was now hanging around with people at work and we would go to the local bar every Thursday and Friday after work.

I started drinking and had become very permisquise. I had also become anorexic. Remember now, I lived on my own so there was no one to tell me to be home at a certain time and no one to make sure that I ate. I basically lived on alcohol. My anorexia started when I met *insert mike*. He was tall and thin. He was the type that could not gain weight no matter how hard he tried. I was 160lbs. and felt fat whenever I was with him. Funny, because I never worried about my weight before. Initially I had lost 40 lbs. in a month. That was because I went to another doctor and had asked for a diet pill. The instructions were to take one pill every two days. I took one pill everyday. I did not know at that time that this particular medication had a narcotic in it. I would run around like a chicken with its head cut off doing not only my job but anyone else's job when they needed help. By time I got home at night, I was too tired to eat. This is how I lost the 40 lbs. so quickly. I liked the way I looked now that I was 120 lbs. so I kept on losing weight. The weight was not coming off as fast as it did earlier so I decided I was not going to eat at all. I had gotten down to 103 lbs. and was very proud of myself. I had discovered a way to rid by body of any food I had ingested. I did not tell anyone what I was doing to myself; they just thought that I was on a diet. I would only eat around other people if I had to. I enjoyed that fact that people would make comments about my weight loss and how good I looked. That was until I got too skinny. Then people just started to worry about me. I liked that. I was the center of attention. I was starving for the attention I did not get as a child.

I was now starting to take this self-harming even further. I would intentionally punch myself in the eye just so that people would notice my black eye and ask me how it happened. I lied and told them I had been mugged. They felt so sorry for me. I relished the attention. Another time I kept scratching at the back of my hand until the skin was off the back of my hand. This time when asked what happened I told everyone the truth. I was upset with my boyfriend and scratching my hand was an unconscious act when I was upset. Guess what? Not one person believed me. They had it in their minds that my boyfriend had done that to me so they would not come around when he was at my apartment.

I was not getting bored with my job. It had become too easy for me. I needed a change. I had requested a transfer to another department just so I could learn something new and be busy again. My boss had given me a raise in hopes that I would stay where I was. However, I was already accepted in the new department. It only took me one month to realize the new job I had was completely boring and did not fill up my days. It was time for me to look for another job.

I was now working for a trucking company. Again, I caught onto the job quickly. There was always something to do so my days were filled again. This company too had changed its name and moved to larger facilities. This company was a family owned company. Working for a family owned company was different to work for. It seemed the harder you worked did not matter. If you were family, you got the raises and you did not have to work as hard as the other employees did in order to get a raise. I worked very hard and was given the title of Supervisor of my department. They had hired a new person for my department and guess what, it was a family member.

I made new friends with my co-workers. A few of us started going to bars and strip clubs. One girl that was in my department lived in a triplex not far from my parent's house. Her parent's were the superintendents. I got a one bedroom where she lived. I found that working for a family owned company they would choose who would be transferred to other departments within the company. I had applied for every opening they had but was passed over every time even though I had proven to them that I was a loyal and hardworking employee. I had now been working for this company about two or three years and being passed up on every opening really got me angry that they would hold me back from advancing. I had expressed interest in the data entry department and was promised I would get the job if an opening came up. I knew the data entry department was stretched because I would go in and help them if I had nothing else to do. Therefore, I knew they needed help but for some reason the company did not expand this department. By now, I was becoming bored again. My job was too easy and there were no more challenges for me. It also seemed that this company was not going to advance me so I decided to quit. By this time, I was married to my first husband and he was making good money. I thought I would take a break from working for a while and just stay at home and relax. I had given this company a months notice because I did not have another job to go to. A girl that had started the same time I did had also given her notice. They accepted her two-week notice but they did not want to accept mine. When I told her they wanted me to stay, she ended up leaving before her two weeks was up. She never liked the fact that we started at the same time and I got the position of Supervisor. Once I gave me notice, the company was trying to get me to stay by promising me the data entry job I wanted years earlier. I told them it was too late for that now. I had enough of working for this company. My boss confided in me and let me know that they did not advance me at work because I was too good at what I did and they wanted to keep me there.

After I left that company, I stayed home for a bit. I was getting tired of working and wanted a break. Well it did not take me long to be bored of staying at home too. I needed structure in my life.

I got another job in a small family owned company. To me this was much better than working for a larger company. There were only about ten of us at this point. As before, I caught onto my new job quickly and again I was helping out others with their jobs. My boss showed his appreciation by giving me a raise every three months until I hit a year. Then I got yearly raises. After about three years, I got bored, so I got another job. However, that job did not suit me well so I went back to the company I just came from. The president had hired his daughter to replace me. She was so happy when I came back because she hated typing. At this time, we were still using carbon paper when typing letters, quotes, sales orders, etc. Not only did you have to correct the typing mistakes on the original you had to correct them on the carbon copy as well. She went through a lot of liquid paper for corrections. Eventually we went to four part carbonless paper. Now you not only had to use white to correct the first sheet, you also had to use yellow, pink, and gold for the rest of the copies. I was hired back to do the typing, accounts receivables and purchasing of office supplies, and back up receptionist.

This company was starting to expand. We were hiring new people all the time. Within five or six years we had gotten so large, we had to move to larger facilities. The company was also expanding by making new departments. They had hired another family member for the new marketing department. They were hiring secretaries for the inside sales department, the outside sales department and the Vice-president also got his own secretary. Each time they hired someone new; a piece of my job would be taken away from me. My only job left now was accounts receivables, purchasing of office supplies and backup receptionist. I no longer had any secretarial jobs that I used to have. My job was getting easier all the time because I had less to do. I again started asking people if they needed any help but because their jobs were not very busy, I had no one to help.

The company was now expanding into different parts of Canada. They opened an office in Quebec, Calgary, and then British Columbia. My workload was increased because I was doing the accounts receivables for all the branch offices as well. This suited me just fine. I would get the orders in a weekly package from the branch offices. I would sort through them and invoice the ones that were shipped. However, since this was only on a weekly basis I had to try to fill the rest of the week with something to do. I was getting bored again but this time things felt different. I had to fight with myself every morning to get up and go to work. I know that I am not the type to stay home and do nothing. I have to stay busy. I have to keep my mind occupied. However, I hated go to work now. I put it down to the fact that I was bored at work and that I just was not being challenged enough but I did not know what to do about it.

During all these years since graduation, my personality kept changing. I was becoming a stronger more dominant personality. I was very out spoken and made people aware of this. I was actually called b**chy. After a while some people would say that I intentionally would start fights because I was a b**ch. That was not true, I actually hated confrontations, but if I knew I was right about something I would go out of my way to prove the other person wrong.

I had changed my personality drastically from when I was a child. I had gone from being a shy introvert to an outspoken extrovert. Another change was that I was no longer self-harming or anorexic. Years earlier I had told my Doctor the truth about what I had been doing to myself.

I had become bored at work again because the company had gotten a new system that streamlined my job to the point that after the first three hours of the day my jobs were done. It was time for me to look for another job. Again I had given a month notice but this time it was because the only other person who could do my job was on vacation for three weeks. I did not have another job to go to I just did not feel that this once small family owned business was good for me anymore, especially since I kept fighting with one of the salesmen, who just happened to be a son of the president.

I ended this job at the end of December 1999 and stayed at home for a few months. I got another job in March 2000 as an office manager of a small company. I enjoyed this very much because it was small and I felt much needed. I managed everything from answering the phones to shipping and everything else in between.

I was always the strong person at work. If anyone needed help, I was there. If anyone needed to know information about a particular item, I would get it for them. If I didn't know the answer, I would research it so I would provide them with the correct information. I am a quick learner. It doesn't matter what job you give me to do, once I have done it a couple of times I would catch on and as a result was able to be left on my own to do my job. I had many people depending on my strength. My bosses at work, my husband, my children, co-workers, siblings, etc.

I was the one people turned to when they wanted the job done right and on time. There were times when co-workers would ask me to get this or that done quickly and to their surprise, I had already done it.

Getting this new job made me realize just how much I hated the company I had just left. I mean not only did I not want to get up in the morning to work I also realized that I hated the people I worked with. Some of us would gossip in the morning until the president came in then we would go to our jobs. During the last year there I stopped sitting in on the gossip. Now I was being accused of being a spy for the president or vice-president. This company and the people I worked with were really beginning to piss me off. I had kept my mouth shut so that there would be no confrontation but it was bottling up inside of me. I remember having mentioned to one girl that I felt like I was walking around with a black cloud above me. It felt like Impending doom. I thought this all meant that there were going to be some big changes within the company because people were starting to be fired even after years of service. Little did I know that the black cloud and Impending doom was for me and only me.

The new company I joined in March 2000 was great at first. Things started to go wrong near the end of that year. Not with me, but with the partners. They were not getting along with each other. One partner decided he wanted it all and he was determined to get it. After the first two years I had told the president I could no longer work with this one particular person and that I wanted to find another job. The president kept assuring me everything would be ok and asked me to hang on. Again my strong personality was getting in the way of some people. The president preferred my strong personality because that meant I could handle things well and would always make sure jobs were done right. I thought this was the Ideal job for me because I was constantly busy and I was also relied upon. One thing did trouble me though. The feeling of Impending doom never left me. I still felt like I was walking around with a black cloud above me. The panic attacks had come back. I was crying for no reason. I was getting angry for no reason. I was mouthy to everyone and I did not care. I had put this all down to the fact that there was one person that I worked with that I could not stand being around.

This was now May 12, 2002 and we had thrown my Mom a huge 80th birthday party at the Legion. Little did we all know that exactly four months later on September 12, 2002 she would be dead from cancer. None of us even knew she had cancer.

In May 2003 I had called my boss at home and told him that I had applied for a job as accounts receivables and receptionist at a company that was only seven minutes away from my home and I was accepted. He did not want me to leave but he understood how I felt. Thinking that a job closer to home would be better for me I was glad that I was accepted. However the black cloud kept following me no matter where I went. I started this new job in hopes that there would be less stress on me since it was close to home. The pay was lousy but I took the job anyway. It only took one week to train me and this was in an industry that I knew nothing about. Almost immediately I knew I was not going to stay at this job very long. It was another family owned business. The owners were paid well while the rest of us got nickled and dimed to death. We were on hourly wages and had to punch a clock and the family was on salary. I felt I should have been put on salary as well since my job was an office job. I had never had to punch a clock before. I had been promised a job and pay review at three months. Well at three months I had to constantly ask for my review. I was handed and envelope and a file with five sheets in it. The envelope was a letter stating that I would not get a pay increase until one year. The file was a review alright, but they wanted me to review myself and then they would discuss the review with me. I was ticked off about the pay raise being declined until the one-year mark, but I had to laugh about the review. Since when does an employee review themselves? I threw this file away and told them it was a joke.

This was now September 2003. The one-year anniversary of my Mothers death. I was driving my daughter's to school one day when I suddenly became enraged with my oldest daughter. I had told her that my key did not open the trunk so she would have to use the button inside the car. I had told her about this a couple of time before. On this particular morning she had tried to use the key to open the trunk to put the backpacks in. I blew up at her so bad that while I was driving the three of us were crying our eyes out. Me out of anger and them because I was saying some pretty mean things to them. My youngest daughter said she could not go to school with her eyes all puffy and red from crying. My oldest daughter agreed with her. So did I. I turned the car around and we all went home. I told them to call it a "Mommy needs me day". The three of us sat on the front step for a long time. All of us trying to figure out what just happened. I cried off and on the whole day. When my Husband got home from work, I explained our day to him. I told him I felt like I just hit a brick wall.

The next day, while driving the girl's to school, I started yelling at them again over a small incident. My oldest daughter said "Mom this is how it started yesterday". She was right. I immediately shut up and dropped the girl's off at their schools. All day I had to hold in the urge to cry or yell. Thank God it was Friday. When I got home the tears kept flowing. My family, as well as myself, was very concerned about what was happening to me. The crying continued into all of Saturday. My Husband was started to get pissed off because I would not stop crying for no reason. That evening, when everyone was asleep, I wrote my husband a letter. I was hoping to express myself in words to him in hopes that he would understand that I was not in control of my emotions. The next day he read the letter. Even though both of us still did not understand what was happening we both tried to work around it. At some point that day, it occurred to me that I was showing signs of depression. I checked it out on the computer. I found a section that mentioned the usual signs of depression. I printed it out to show my husband. I checked off most of the symptoms and I added my own symptoms from what I was going through. Once I realized it was depression I almost felt relief. Now I knew what was happening to me. Fortunately I was now on a week's vacation. I called my Doctor first thing Monday morning and booked an appointment for Wednesday. My husband came with me because he did not want me driving. He also wanted to understand what was happening. Had I diagnosed my correctly?

My Doctor read my list I printed off and gave me a quick look. I definitely had depression. This diagnosis also came as a surprise to my Doctor because he always knew me to be the strong, take charge, no nonsense type of person. He put me on Remeron and told me to take time off work to let the drug start to work and to get plenty of sleep. The next day I went into work to explain my situation. They completely understood. One of the owners has a son who suffers from depression. They told me to take a month off and to always take my medication.

I figured I would be back at work in two weeks. Wrong. It did take a month for me to start feeling human again. My boss said I could come in on a part-time basis until I felt strong enough to go back on full-time. I did about three weeks of part-time then went back to full-time. This was now the beginning of October 2003. Everything was going along fine. I was even starting to have fun with my family. I remember telling my boss near the end of October that I felt like the depression was starting all over again. I had always taken my medication as directed but I felt something was not right.

It was now November 2003 and not only had the depression come back, something else had come along with it. RAGE! I remember not going into work one Monday and I didn't even bother to call work and tell them. I did however, call them on Tuesday, and told them I did not know when I was coming back to work. I explained about the rage. Since I was front receptionist I did not think it would be a wise decision to come back yet. I had to get the rage under control first. I told them I had a Doctor's appointment on Friday morning and that I would call them after that. Well I never made it out of the Doctor's office on my own. The rage was so bad this particular day. I had dropped the girl's off at school and was heading home. The driver in front of me was so slow I felt like ramming his car to help push him along. However, I didn't. I kept telling myself to just go home. This slow driver was really getting on my nerves. At the stop sign by my house I thought "good, I hope this guy goes straight through instead of turning. I had to make a left to get onto my street. This driver made a left hand turn. UGH! Now I was really enraged. I am glad I help my rage in check because it turned out to be my neighbor. I parked and went into the house to relax before my Doctor's appointment.

I went to my appointment. By now I had built up so much rage that I was speaking through clenched jaws. I was not making eye contact. I was very rude to the Doctor. I even told him that when I leave I could not promise that I wouldn't harm myself or someone else. OOPS! Not supposed to say that to a Doctor. (Continued in Chapter 12).

Chapter 9
My First Marriage

I met my first husband, Robert when I was twenty-two years old and shortly after breaking up with "Chris". Robert was a DJ and a friend of mind was having a New Years Eve party. Robert was the DJ at this party. We started talking and ended up dating shortly after the party. It was approximately a year of dating when we moved in together. We had a small one-bedroom apartment in the basement of a house. We had a lot of fun together. He had many friends. It seemed that no matter where we went, someone knew him. One night when we went out to have dinner and play pool, a man approached me and said, "You can tell you two are in love by the way you look at each other". He was right. Robert was a great person and fun to be around.

In September 1984, we got married. He had changed jobs so we left the basement apartment and moved into a one bedroom in a triplex closer to his work and not too far away from my Parents. Everything was going great until September 1985 when we were invited to the wedding of one of his cousins in Kingston, Ontario. The day we were getting ready for the wedding, I was in the bathroom drying my hair and out of the corner of my eye, and I saw Robert fall straight back and starting to have a seizure. He had never had seizure before so this scared the crap out of me. I immediately called his cousin who immediately rushed over to where we were staying. He was going so fast the police stopped him. After explaining why he was going so fast, the officers followed him to where we were. The police then called 911. He was taken to the hospital for tests. After the test results came back, the Doctor told me he did not have epilepsy. All blood work was normal. They could not explain why he had the seizure. They kept him in the hospital for a couple of hours and had him on IV.

When they released him, we went back to where we were staying to get ready for the wedding. We got to the wedding just as they were finishing dinner. They made up a couple of plates for us. When we were finished eating there was a couple of speeches and then the wedding was over. They were not having a reception. We went out that night with some of his other cousins to a bar to have a few drinks and dance. The more Robert drank the better he felt.

We left to go home the next day and as out luck would have it, the car we rented broke down. This was on a Sunday and nothing was open. One of his cousins was a tow truck driver and even he couldn't touch it on a Sunday. We ended up leaving it at the side of the road and contacted the OPP to let them know it was there. His Aunt and cousin drove us home. We contacted the place where we rented the car, they went, and had it towed back to Toronto. It turned out that the thermostat was seized and the car had overheated on us. Boy that weekend was just full of seizures.

Robert continued to have seizures and each time the Doctor could not figure out why. It had occurred to me that the more Robert drank the better he would feel. If he did not have a certain amount of alcohol in his system he would seize. That was when I realized I was married to an alcoholic. I tried for the next couple of years to get him some help. I had him in different hospitals but each time he came out he would sneak drinks from any source he could get it from. He would practically down a whole bottle of NyQuil. He drank my Vodka and replaced it with water. He would go to the corner store and buy Bitters. He could not keep a job. He would buy little bottles of alcohol from the liquor store and hide them in the couch.

In January 1987 I became pregnant. I was still trying to get Robert sobered up but I also had my own health to think of. We had a daughter in October 1987. I was on maternity leave for four months. When I went back to work, I had arranged for one of my sister's to come to my apartment every morning and pick my daughter up and take her back to her place. I would pick my daughter up from there every night.

I had always told Robert that you should never leave a baby alone, not even to run to the corner store. Well that was exactly what he did. When my sister came to pick up my daughter one morning, she could hear my daughter crying but Robert was not answering the door. I had given a key to my sister. She was just about to open the door when she saw Robert come upstairs.

He had gone to the corner store to buy cigarettes. My sister did not want to tell me about this.

It took her about a month before she told me what had happened. I immediately kicked him out of the apartment to go live with his alcoholic Father. It was only after I moved out that some of the old neighbor's told me that my daughter would be crying constantly whenever I was not home.

I moved back in with my Parents. Robert and his Father took our old apartment. I had gone to a lawyer's to seek a divorce. Robert did not contest anything. He had supervised visitation at my Parents house every second Sunday. For a while he would come with his Father for visitations. I did not object to his Father coming over, after all she was his one and only Grandchild. His Father had sobered up by this time and was now in charge of trying to sober up his Son.

During one of the visitations Roberts, naturally, had been drinking and therefore his co-ordination was off. He ended up tripping our daughter and she fell into the coffee table. I immediately went to my lawyer and had him draw up papers stating that if Robert had even one drink before coming over for visitation my lawyer would have his visitations revoked. Robert never showed up after that. I guess he decided that he would rather stay at home and drink then visit his daughter. Her Grandfather kept up the visitations though. I did not want to stop him from watching his Granddaughter grow up. Unfortunately, he passed away when she was about four years old. At least she had some time with her Grandfather.

Our divorce had gone through on her second birthday. By this time, I was now dating Ian, my current husband.

Ten years later I got a phone call from the police asking if I was married to Robert. I told them I had and they told me that he was found dead in his apartment. Apparently he was going through dialysis and his nurse got worried when he missed a couple of appointments. She called the police and that was when they found him. I don't know how long he had been there by himself and I didn't ask.

I let our daughter, who was now ten years old, make all the arrangements for the funeral. After all, it was her Father. The people at the funeral home were great to her. She picked out some clothes for him; she also gave them a couple of pictures of Robert and asked if they could make him look like the pictures. We didn't know exactly how far Robert had fallen. When the funeral home received his body, they knew immediately that there was no way they could make him look like any of the pictures. They did the best they could and my daughter didn't complain.

The funeral home gave her an easel so she could make a collage of pictures. They really treated her great and took great care with her on the day of the funeral. They had to ask her a couple of time if it was OK to close the coffin. She finally said yes after the third time they asked her. That was that. Her Father was gone. Dead at the age of thirty-eight.

Chapter 10
My Current Marriage

My current husband Ian is my soul mate. It is actually quite funny. We knew each other since we were kids. His sister is married to my brother. I had spent a summer with my brother's family and Ian lived next door. We hung around that summer. We would go swimming every afternoon. I was 12 and he was 11.

I had started divorce proceedings with my first Husband in early 1988. December 1988 I had no one to go with me to my company Christmas party. Our mutual Nephew was living at my Parent's house with me at that time. My Nephew asked me if I wanted to ask Uncle Ian to go to the party with me. I said sure, why not. I had not seen Ian since 1972 and back then I made fun of him because he had big ears and love handles. The man that walked in the door to pick me up was definitely not the little kid I remember. He was now over 6ft. tall and had grown into a very handsome man.

I must admit though that I was not very nice to him that night. I didn't like the way he danced so I told him that if he wanted to dance there was plenty of other women to dance with. Well he did not think too highly of me after that.

Not one to give up, our Nephew arranged for us to go on a date. It was over Christmas time and my daughter was not feeling too well. Ian thought I was just trying to get out of going on a date with him. It was not until our Nephew confirmed that my daughter was sick and I was not making up a story.

We finally got together and went to a movie then bowling. Funny thing, we met a couple of our other Nephews at the movies. We both like to bowl, and eventually ended up joining a bowling league together. It turned out we had a lot in common and the more I got to know him the more I felt that this man was definitely my soul mate. We were destined to be together.

My daughter and I moved in with Ian in March of 1989. We got married in February 1990 and had a daughter in July 1991.

Not too long after our marriage, I started to have panic attacks. Whenever we were driving somewhere Ian would do the driving, especially on highways. I had the feeling that we were going to be hit by another driver. I was fine whenever I was the driver because I would take the back roads to get anywhere. Sure, it took me longer to get anywhere but I felt safer on the road less traveled.

My panic attacks were so bad at times, that it would cause arguments between Ian and me. I just could not control it. I would bawl my eyes out sometimes. I would even ask Ian to pull over so I could get out of the car. He thought this was ridiculous. I remember times when I begged him to get off the highway at the next exit and take the side roads. This went on for years. I think it started near the end of 1990. I went to the Doctor and explained what was happening to me. That was when I was diagnosed with panic attacks.

My Doctor originally put me on medication but I did not want to be dependant on any medication for an extended period. I took what was originally dispensed to me but never repeated the prescription. I ended up suffering with these panic attacks on my own for years. Relatives kept telling me to get some serious help because my attacks were so bad that nobody wanted to drive me anywhere. They kept telling me that there has to be some sort of medication that would help me. I ignored them. I didn't think the attacks for last for years, but they did. Sometimes my children would joke around in the car and say things like "Dad, look out there's a car a mile ahead, put on your breaks". Even I had to laugh when they came out with jokes like that.

A lot of things were happening to me at this time. It was not only the panic attacks. I would start crying for no reason anytime of the day. I would get the urge to cry just driving to work. I put it down to the fact that I hated going to work. Not that I hated my job, it was just the fact that I had to drive to work. Almost every evening I would have a fear of getting into the car to go to work the next day and getting into an accident just because I did not trust other drivers. I lost a lot of sleep over this too.

Ian and I were married for about six years when I started to feel trapped in my marriage. Trapped as a Mother. Trapped having to go to work. Just overall trapped. Nothing new was happening in my life. I had decided to take up sewing. I would make summer dresses and hats for my daughters. One night I had asked Ian if he could start making the lunches for the next day. I was starting to put away my sewing for the night. I could not believe my ears when Ian said that I should not do my sewing until after my "chores" were done. Well I flipped. I went on a rampage. I started punching the walls. I would go up to every laundry basket and empty it on the floor and then throw the baskets around the rooms. I even slapped Ian across the face. When he raised his hand to me I said, "Are you going to slap me back. Go ahead then, I don't care". He never would hit me and I knew it. We would have stupid fights like this and it frightened my daughters each time because I was out of control. They would ask if we were going to get divorced.

It got to the point where Ian and I would not even talk to each other for about a week. It would be up to him to start a conversation with me to straighten out our problems because I certainly was not going to make the first move.

Ian had started to look for apartments because we just could not live together anymore. After about a month and a half of looking, we sat down and talked things over. He told me that if I thought he was not going to date again then I was wrong. I only wanted him to move out so that we could start dating again and hoped to rekindle the spark we used to have. When he told me he might date again, I felt like I had just been kicked in the face. That was not at all what I wanted. Ian saying that made me realize that I do love this man with all my heart. What the heck was I throwing my marriage away for? I looked good and hard at myself then. What was wrong with me? We talked for a long time and I told him how I really felt. I did not want him to leave. I needed him. He was my strength. He was my best friend. He was my soul mate. All of this hit me at once and I could not apologize enough to him. I really needed to convince him that I meant what I said. If he had not of said those works to me, I don't know if we would be divorced by now or not. However, I am glad he told me how he felt.

Now our marriage was back on track. We both realized that we not only loved each other but we both needed each other. We made each other stronger. We started having fun again. The most important thing is that we made our daughters feel secure that our marriage was solid.

The panic attacks were still with me but he was calmer with me in the car now. I really did try hard not to panic but it always got the best of me. He understood I could not help it and kept telling me to go to the Doctor's to do something about it. Of course I didn't. Even when I was not feeling well, I would not go to the Doctor's until I had to. I just could not be bothered.

During all this time I was hearing TV's and radio stations even though I knew that everyone was in bed and there was no TV or radio on. Of course, I did not tell anyone of this because it had been happening to me for several years. I would hear my name being called with no one around. I would sense something or someone with me when Ian was working late. I would see black dots out of the corner of my eyes.

Now that our marriage was back on track, I started to tell Ian about the things I saw, felt, and heard. He just thought I was under a lot of stress because he knew I hated to go to work everyday.

Just to let you all know my marriage is still going strong. Ian and I have been married for eighteen years now. We are so much closer today than both of us ever thought we would be. We miss each other when we are not together.

Our song used to be "Patience" by Guns N Roses. Our song now is "Truly, Madly, Deeply" by Savage Garden.

Chapter 11
My Children

My pregnancy of my first child was uneventful except for the fact that I could no longer stand to eat cheese and I used to have cheese almost every day.

The birth however, was a completely different story. The Doctor's and Nurses' could not find a heartbeat no matter how they tried. When they shook my stomach, they could find a faint heartbeat and then it would go away again. They had me get up and walk around then when I got back in bed, they could find a heartbeat, but again it would go away. I ended up having to have a continual epidural so that I could not feel contractions. I was at the hospital at 1:00am and didn't give birth until 4:40pm that afternoon. In all that time, they kept checking to see if there was still a heartbeat. Just before I gave birth, I had a reaction to the epidermal so they immediately pulled me into an emergency room.

There was another woman giving birth at the same time and I remember the Anesthetist asking my Doctor which mother she should freeze first. My Doctor said to freeze me first because there may be fetal distress. I remember this hit me like a brick. I said to myself, I can't believe that I carried this baby full term and that it may not survive the birth. My Doctor was using an instrument that guides the baby's head when she told me to push. I pushed so hard that she had to tell me to stop because I practically pushed the baby out completely. I heard the baby cry and the Doctor held her up and said, "You gave us quite a scare". She then held the baby up in front of me and I remember saying "she had nice earlobes for earrings". What a thing to think. My baby was perfectly fine. The cord was not wrapped around her neck at all she was just asleep. Every time they tried to find a heartbeat they would wake her up by having me walk around but then she would go back to sleep, which is why they couldn't detect a strong heartbeat. She was fine and she was healthy. She pinked up almost immediately.

They put me in another bed and I said goodbye to my baby thinking they were putting her in the nursing room. The nurse's laughed and said she's not going anywhere. She's staying with you for a while. Therefore, they wrapped her up, put her in the crook of my left arm, and wheeled me to the recovery room.

After talking to and singing to my baby, I was tired and I just wanted someone to take the baby away from me. I finally got up enough nerve to push the button for the nurse. When she came in, I asked her if she could take the baby and she replied that she was just about to do that before I buzzed her.

It took me four days to realize that I loved my baby. I did not immediately become attached. In 1987, they would allow you to stay in the hospital for 5 days, the baby was not in the room during visiting hours, but to show the baby to my visitors I was the one that had to go into the nursing station and show my child myself. They wouldn't even let me leave the hospital until I had been shown how to bathe a baby. They used my daughter as the child to show other new Mother's how to bathe a baby. I was sitting in this class. My daughter grabbed hold of the side railing and was beginning to pull her self over when the nurse looked back. She said wow babies aren't supposed to be able to do that at three days old. Then she proceeded to warn us to keep one hand on a child while you get their bath ready or have to turn your head away from them for any reason. There was quite a chuckle in the class.

When I finally took the baby home, I was a bit afraid but I tried my best. It seemed that while I was in the hospital, I had no problem breast-feeding but when I got home, I couldn't. This baby was a demand feeder. I ended up putting her on a bottle because I just couldn't do anything for her anymore. I could not each cheese while pregnant with her and now she loves all dairy products. I can eat cheese again.

My husband was of no help to me. I grew up with many children around so I had some idea of how to handle a baby. He was an only child so he felt uncomfortable. He didn't even know how to hold a baby.

My second pregnancy was as uneventful as my first. This pregnancy I could not stand to eat or smell chicken and chicken was a big part of my diet. Again, I was at the hospital at 1:00am however, this child was not waiting for any Doctor to deliver her. She had her own agenda. I kept telling the nurses that the baby was coming but they kept saying, "You are not dilated enough yet". I insisted that the child was coming. One nurse said that if the baby came early she was qualified to deliver. After more insistence by me, they finally checked. Sure enough, the baby was crowning, which shocked both nurses.

The Doctor showed up just in time to guide the baby out. My second daughter was born at 1:50am. Less than an hour after I entered the hospital. In the last month of this pregnancy, I craved fruit and any cookie that had nuts in it. This daughter loved fruit and cookies as well as chicken.

I remember thinking that this was going to be a child that will insist on having her own way no matter what. Just like her birth. She is a very funny kid. Whenever she hurt herself, all I had to do was give her a cookie and all was right with the world again. As the terrible twos carried into the trying threes, I realized that the terrible twos was not a phase she was going through. It was her personality. She is very stubborn. It took me approximately two weeks to fall in love with this child. Every time I was feeding her I would look down at her and think, I know this is my child but it feels more like I am babysitting someone else's child. She never was a child to be coddled. I was extremely happy when I did finally fall in love with her.

For both of my daughter's I made up songs just for them. Each song ended with Robert Munch "I'll Love you forever, I'll like you for always, as long as I'm living my baby you'll me". Both my daughters still remember their songs even though they are both teenagers now.

My oldest daughter has always been the type of person that would go out of her way to help anyone. She is like a psychiatrist to her friends but gets overwhelmed with their problems that I let her vent out on my. Now that I understand my illness, I try my hardest to talk to her because I think she could possible end up like me because she cannot help taking on other people's problems.

My youngest daughter just goes through her life, so far, enjoying hanging out with her friends. Like my oldest, my youngest has a very strong personality. They both do not let anyone push them around.

I made a promise to myself that if I had any children I was not going to treat them the way my Mother treated me. If my girls have any questions about anything, I made sure I answered them honestly. I explained to both of them what to expect from their bodies during different stages of their lives.

Even when I was pregnant the second time, my oldest would ask me questions about how to feed a new baby. I fully explained it to her even though she was only three years old. I believe in being honest and open with all children. I think this is why my kids understood the lack of emotion I showed them and my Husband when I was hospitalized. Even though I hurt their feelings and made them cry, they knew it was not really their Mother talking. It was my illness.

At points in their lives as they were growing up, they did see another side of me that showed rage. However, these spells dissipated as quickly as they came. During these times, I said and did some pretty awful stuff.

Chapter 12
My First Breakdown and Hospitalization

I was now stuck in my Doctors office until either I had someone pick me up and take me to the hospital, or I get a police to take me. I was now no longer to drive because I had threatened to use my vehicle as a means to kill myself. My license wasn't taken away; I was just not allowed to drive until my Doctor gave me the OK. My Doctor contacted my sister and she came to pick me up and take me to the hospital.

Please understand that at this point, I had no expression on my face, I was in a rage mood, I was saying mean things to people, and I just didn't care if I lived or died.

My doctor had called the hospital ahead of time so they expected me. I was put into a room where a crisis counselor spoke to me. I told him that I didn't feel anything. When he left, an ER Doctor came in to talk to me. I told him the same things I had told the counselor. I waited another half hour after the ER

Doctor left then I told my sister that I wanted to leave. I didn't feel like hanging around the hospital anymore. She knew that I shouldn't leave in the condition I was in so she went to talk to the ER Doctor. The Doctor then handed me a piece of paper. I didn't even bother to read it. I didn't care what it said I just wanted to leave. I saw the crisis counselor in the hall so I asked him if I could go now. I showed him what the Doctor gave me and he sat me back down in the crisis room. I hadn't really noticed a security guard standing beside me. The counselor told me that the piece of paper meant that I surrendered my rights to leave and that I was going to be admitted. I just didn't care anymore. They put me in the room beside the security guards office so they could keep an eye on me. My sister had to leave to pick up my kids from school and then pick my husband up at the GO Station. She explained everything to them then had to take my husband to my Doctors office to pick up my car.

I was taken to the hospital at approx. 1:00 in the afternoon and my family came in at 6:00 pm. My husband had brought me a coffee and my cigarettes. There were many tears. I think it shocked everyone the lack of expression on my face. I was making my daughters as well as my husband cry because of the things I was saying to them. I was telling them that I wanted to die.

I was now going to be admitted into the Psych Ward for a minimum of 10 days. As the word spread throughout my family, a lot of them were shocked and never expected this of me because I had become a strong personality. A few family members (besides my husband and kids) came to visit me. This showed me which of my siblings actually cared about whether I lived or died.

Now that I was admitted, a couple of different physiatrists' came to talk to me. I didn't find they helped me at all. I was still confused about the last couple of months leading up to this point. At this time, I was only diagnosed as depressed with suicidal tendencies. They had put me on some heavy-duty drugs. On my second day there, the psychiatrist came in and tried to wake me up. I didn't hear or feel a thing. I was out for the count. When I finally woke up the Doctor had come back to see me. He said it was good that I slept so long and so soundly because my brain needed to sleep. After three days, I had gotten used to the place and I actually felt at home. I felt like this was where I belonged. After seven days they let me go home for the weekend but I had to be back in the hospital by 6:00 pm Sunday evening. It felt good to be home for a bit. I went back to the hospital on Sunday evening. The next day the psychiatrist asked me how everything went on the weekend. I told him that all went well. I no longer had suicidal thoughts and I felt good. He then told me I was allowed to go home for good. I immediately called my husband and told him to come pick me up. I was going home. I psych ward no longer felt like home to me. I hope I never have to end up there again.

I can't say everyday has been easy since being released. I have had more breakdowns. Sometimes I know what is happening and that was when I would go and have a nap. However, there were other times when it hit me so quickly I was even stumped. Over time, my Doctor has had to increase my medications accordingly.

Even under my Doctors care, I still had breakdowns. Nothing is a sure thing. Over the years, though I have begun to understand my illness. My family has too. They can just look at my face and they would know something was not right. The suicidal thoughts have diminished over the years but I still have moments of rage.

Chapter 13
Living With Depression

Now I was seeing things, hearing voices, people asking me questions, feeling things that I could not see.

For example my oldest daughter asked me a questions and I automatically responded with "not right now dear" before I realized she was at school.

My youngest daughter called "Mom" just after my oldest asked me the above question, so I knew right away that my youngest was still in school too.

My Fathers face came into my mind. Full details of what he looked like, not just a partial or even a blurred vision. A complete vision of him.

One of my older sisters phoned me and asked how I was doing. I told her I was fine then there was dead air on the phone. I kept repeating "hello" before I even realized the phone never even rang.

I feel a presence around me and on the other side of my bed even though I know there is no one there. I can feel the other side of my bed indent as if someone was sitting beside me. I felt my left shoulder being rubbed very, very gently a couple of time.

I was sitting in the living room with no TV on and I heard someone say "Howdy Fellas". I looked out the window to see if my neighbor was outside but there was no one there.

I heard a Beatles song in its entirety, full instrumentals and all but, I had no radio on. Once the song was over that was it, I heard no more music. The next day, in a different part of the house, I heard another song (can't remember the artist or name of the song) and again, there was no radio on. Just like the Beatles song, I heard it in its entirety, instruments, and all.

I woke up one morning seeing my husband standing at the bedroom door fully dressed but he had a cowboy hat in his hand. This was at 7:00am and my husband was already at work for the day.

I heard my husband call my name even though I knew he was at work. I hear telephones ringing but they sound like they are in a distance.

My whole body jerks just as I am about to fall asleep. It feels almost like a convulsion. Sometimes I wake up and am unsure of my surroundings.

One day I had a buzzing in my right ear, and then the buzzing traveled down my right arm. It was as if I had bees all over my right side of my body. When I mentioned this to the Doctor, he sent me to a specialist because he was unsure of whether this was a part of the disorder or something else going on in my brain. I went to the specialist and he asked me a few questions while he did a check up. Then he asked me if my whole body jumped when I was falling asleep. I was astounded when he asked me that. I hadn't even told my Doctor that. I told him that my body did jump and he then reassured me that I was not having convulsions. I didn't even tell him that I thought I was having convulsions. It was as if he read my mind.

One time, when I was sleeping, I saw decks of playing cards floating around near the ceiling of my bedroom. This woke me up. I wondered what that meant. When I shut my eyes, again I saw a bird floating in the corner of my bedroom. It was red but it looked like it was origami. I opened my eyes again and tried to figure out what was happening. Again, I shut my eyes and this time I saw three white elephants with three black dots on each one, floating on my banister. This was when I decided I was getting out of bed so I wouldn't see anymore strange things floating.

I heard a radio station and I thought it might have been my kids or my husband with the radio on. They were all still in bed and I was in the den alone. When they woke up, I asked each of them if they had a radio on but none of them did.

I heard my husband ask me a question and instinctively I answered him before I realized he was at work.

Now at this point I'm sure all of this was happening to me because I was on medication that my body wasn't used to. I figured after a while all this would stop so I didn't let any of it bother me.

January 12, 2004 – My Doctor increased my Effexor from 75mg's to 150 mg's to control my moods. I was still having uncontrolled moods.

January 17, 18, 19, & 20, 2004 – I have had some numbness in my fingertips (especially the thumb) in my left hand. This concerns me because I am left handed. I made a note to tell my Doctor about this because it happened four days in a row.

January 21, 2004 – I was just about to go for a nap at 10:00am when I heard someone come into the house. I heard them take off their shoes and walk around the house. I thought it was my oldest daughter coming home after her exam but it was strange because she told me her exam was at 10:00am. I was a little afraid but figuring it was my daughter I went to sleep. When my husband called me, I told him our daughter must have been home and went back out because when I got up she was not home. She got home at 2:10pm and I asked her if she had been home. She told me that she had just gotten out of her exam. This is freaking me out. I checked around the house but there were no signs of anyone being there and nothing was missing. Even the door was locked when I checked it.

January 25, 2004 – I contemplated suicide again today. My husband was harping on me about our bills and he doesn't know if we can afford to keep the house. I told him I was sorry that I was sick and on EI benefits. The benefits would run out next month and he told me I might not qualify for CPP. He was pushing me to get a job. I couldn't take it anymore and I went for a walk. I was thinking that if I just walked over to Highway 410 and were hit by a vehicle all of our problems would be solved. I hope that I would die and he would get my life insurance benefits. He wouldn't have a sick wife to worry about, the mortgage would be paid off, and he would have no more money problems. He could also apply for CPP for survivor's benefits. I came so close but the thought of how devastating it would be for the driver stopped me. I don't want to hurt anyone except myself. I just wanted to end all this misery. Just how sick am I? Am I sicker than I thought I was?

January 28, 2004 – Today, I felt a presence sit on my bed beside me.

January 29, 2004 – Today, I felt a presence lay beside me this time. I seem to feel this presence around me when I am or seem to be at my lowest point.

February 2, 2004 – My Doctor increased my seraqual to 100mg's to help my brain sleep better.

February 25, 2004 – I told my Doctor that I still wasn't sleeping well and that I was having Psychotic episodes again. I was also seeing my Dad again.

March 3, 2004 – My Doctor increased my seraqual but this time to 300 mg's.

March 24, 2004 – I saw my Mom come off an airplane and then I saw one of my sisters hand wave at my Mom. Strange thing was that it was my hand I saw waving but for some reason I was my sister. My Mom was in full color but nobody else around her was. It was also a vision of my Mom when she was much younger.

March 29, 2004 – I woke up this morning and was hearing a full announcement of a hockey game. I knew this wasn't a dream because it continued as I got dressed for the day. I have been hearing hockey games for several years even without the TV being on.

March 30, 2004 – My youngest always listens to music when she is on the computer. I knew she had gone up to her bedroom but I thought she would be right down so I let her music continue. After about 10 minutes, I went up and asked her to go downstairs and turn off her music on the computer especially since she was now watching TV in her room. She told me she had already turned off the music but to make me happy she went downstairs to check. Her music was not only off but she also logged off the computer. Then she said to me "Mom you're hearing things again".

April 2, 2004 – I heard a voice saying "you're late this morning aren't you"? I immediately woke up and saw that it was 6:45am and I normally wake up at 6:00am. After I got my daughter off to school, I went back to bed. I couldn't fall asleep because I could hear someone playing the flute. Only my youngest plays the flute but she was still asleep. I then checked all the clock radios and not one of them was on. Why do I go for periods with no occurrences, then all of a sudden I start seeing and hearing things again? I felt troubled by this.

April 24, 2004 – I am hearing music again and no one is home with me. This time it is rap and it sounds like it's coming from a distance but still in the house somewhere.

May 10, 2004 – Today, I woke up feeling on edge and angry. I don't know why because I didn't go to bed mad at anyone or anything. These feelings stayed with me for the entire week and my Husband was getting very worried because he said I had the same stone look on my face as I did when I was in the hospital. I don't know why I had this setback or even why it lasted a whole week. My husband asked me to do nothing but relax and take it easy. I took his advise and when I woke up the following Saturday I felt normal again (well as normal as I could feel anyway). Why would I have had this setback?

May 22, 2004 – I have been feeling sad and down lately and anger very easy. My husband said I have been tossing, turning, and thrashing around in my sleep. I don't remember any of it of course. I have been hearing voices again but this time the voice was not anyone I know. I just hear people talking but they are not talking to me, they are having their own conversations around me. I can see people in a big circle and they are talking to each other. I'm standing in the middle continually looking over my left shoulder because someone is calling my name. This voice has been calling my name for some time now but every time I look around there was nobody there. I told one of my sisters about this. She told me that if it happens again ask this person what it is they want from you. I thought that was a great idea, so next time I heard my name called I asked the question. I got no reply. However, my name was not being called anymore. Whomever it was teasing me has now stopped.

June 3, 2004 – My Doctor increased my seroquel to 400mg's.

June 16, 2004 – My Husband is finding it increasingly difficult to sleep with me because I thrash about so much. He's not sure but he thinks that sometimes I am even crying in my sleep.

June 21, 2004 – Again I hear my Husband talking to me even though I know he is at work.

June 16, 2004 – I am still hearing radios and televisions.

June 28, 2004 – My Husband finally had enough of trying to sleep with me. He set up the futon in our bedroom so he can get some sleep. I don't know what I do at night but I do wake up sometimes with bruises on my legs especially around my knees. I got up one night to go to the bathroom and was disoriented. I headed for the window. I turned around and headed for the door and hit my ankle on the bed frame, which woke my Husband up. I don't remember going to the bathroom and I don't remember getting back into bed but that is what my Husband said I did. I must have been sleep walking which I find somewhat funny because I have never slept walked before.

June 29, 2004 – Today I was in the kitchen sewing when all of a sudden I could hear a TV on as clear as a bell as if someone in turned on the TV. I was home alone so this freaked me a bit. Usually when I hear a radio or TV it is very faint and sounds like it is coming from another room. This was loud as if I was in the same room but I wasn't.

Chapter 14
Living With Bi-Polar

June 30, 2004 – Again today, I was hearing the TV turned up loud. This is about 8:30 in the morning. Earlier I heard music turned up loud too. Both of my children are still asleep and Ian had left for work. I am starting to hear familiar voices talking to me and asking me questions again. Ian in particular, even though I have heard my daughter's and sisters as well.

Last time I saw my Doctor he had said to me "oh, that's just your bi-polar". All this time I thought I was just suffering from depression. I didn't know I had already been diagnosed as bi-polar. So there it was I am Bi-Polar.

July 1, 2004 – Apparently I was sleep walking again. The girl's said I came downstairs at 1:30 in the morning (yes they were still awake) and I asked them to go to bed. My oldest said I was whimpering or crying (she couldn't tell) then I walked right into the banister and went back upstairs to bed. I don't remember doing any of this. I also don't remember having any dreams since being put on medication but one night I woke up frightened because in my dream I was being lowered on a ladder into the ocean with a shark below me. I was told to keep climbing the ladder to avoid the shark but the rigging broke on the ship and it sent me and the ladder down into the ocean. I didn't even have any diving gear or oxygen tank on.

July 3, 2004 – Today Ian and I went to Canadian Tire and while he was getting a hotdog, I decided to go and load up the car then go and pick him up. We then went to The Home Depot. Ian couldn't believe how fast I was driving, zipping in and out of traffic. On a couple of occasions (with my daughter in the car), I had changed lanes and she commented on the fact that I was close to the cars when I changed lanes. I now started to take highways and I keep up or go faster than the traffic ahead. Ian told my oldest about the way I am driving now and that I even made him nervous. One day when she was in the car with me, she told me what her Dad had said about my driving habits. I realize that when the cars in front of me are not going as fast as I would like them to I zip in and out of traffic. I feel anger build up in me when the cars ahead of me are going slow. I know my driving habits have changed but I am always in control of my vehicle. I was told to stop driving again by my Doctor or else he would have my license taken away. I had to obey to this because I did not want to lose my license. I started riding my bike instead. If I had go to anywhere far or even to go shopping, Ian drove me.

July 5, 2004 – Today was a very blah day. I couldn't get up any energy to do any of my many projects I have on the go. I kept going back to bed instead. I finally got up at 2:30 in the afternoon and had a shower. I had opened all the windows because there was a nice breeze outside. After my shower, I was dressed and sat on my couch in the living room. The couch is located in front of the sliding back doors. The breeze felt good on my face and the house was nice and quite (considering there were a number of children in the house). While I was sitting there, thinking how nice the breeze was, a thought came into my head. I thought, "Wow I could just slit my throat right now. No better yet, with my arm hanging over the back of the couch, I could slit my left wrist and it would take a while before anyone would be able to spot the blood". Why did I have a sudden thought of violence when I was in a peaceful state of mind? It made me remember a recurring dream I had when I was in my mid twenties. I would be dreaming about driving along peacefully on a bright beautiful day when all of a sudden I was hit head on by a truck. Both dreams happened in two different locations, both jolted my out of my sleep by the sudden impact of violence. Both scared me enough to remember them after all this time. I also had another recurring dream. A man was standing at my bedside with a big black dog beside him. It wasn't the man I was afraid of it was the dog. The dog would talk to me and sounded threatening. I know, I know, yes it was the dog talking. I have no idea what this dream is all about, but I do know it frightened me. The only thing I can think of is that I have always been and still am afraid of dogs.

Both Ian and Holly are sensitive to my facial expressions even if I'm not aware of it myself. They don't like what they have been seeing lately. I have a stone look on my face and I show no emotions.

July 30, 2004 – My Doctor has increased my seraquil to 600 mg's and confirmed that I am Bi-Polar. I had to ask him again just to see if he still considered me bi-polar. I still hear voices, which is why he increased my medication again. Apparently, my brain is still not getting enough sleep.

August 16, 2004 – My left arm has been sore from my shoulder down to my elbow. It felt like the muscles were contracting. If I have my hand up (either arm), my fingers go numb until I put my hands down. Even if I am gripping an item for some time, my fingers will go numb on the hand that is doing the gripping. I have noticed lately too, that if I raise both arms above my head I feel nausea and dizziness. I have to put my arms down and stay still until it passes. At night (usually about an hour after I have gone to bed), my left leg muscles contract from the top of my thigh to the knee. What I do to relieve this is get up and walk around but that has become almost dangerous since I still have the medication in me and I am very groggy. Sometime Ian will wake up and help me get up and down the stairs. Once I have walked around, I can go back to bed and will sleep peacefully until the morning.

October 15, 2004 – I am still having problems with my left arm. My first physio appointment is October 18th. My left leg still goes numb but now it is happening every night. When I do hand sewing my left hand goes numb at the fingertips. Another thing that is happening to me is a crushing pain in my chest. It feels like someone is sitting on my chest. When this first occurred, it was just after I had taken my medication for the evening. I thought that maybe some pills were stuck so I drink some more water and the pain goes away. The next two times this happened was when I was trying to take an afternoon nap. I hadn't taken any medications so I know that was not the problem. This time though, after drinking more water the pain was still there. I couldn't take it anymore so I got up. The pain then would just become a dull pain. On another occasion when I was having an afternoon nap, I would literally be jolted out of bed because the paid felt like something sharp had just pierced into my heart.

When I saw my Doctor on Oct. 25th, he asked me how I was. I believe I said "blah". My Doctor told me many of his patients feel that way because of the weather, but I knew it wasn't the weather that was affecting me. I have not been able to sleep as much as I usually do. Even after I take my medication at night, it takes me about 1 1/2 hours to get to sleep. Because of this, I have been having a lot of psychotic episodes and even hallucinations.

Not only do I hear my family talking to me, I also hear many other people talking to me. Some voices I recognize and others I don't. It seems that when my mind is Idle I hear things. I also hear my front door open and I can hear heavy footsteps but when I go to check there is no one there. Either I hear the door then the footsteps or sometimes it's the footsteps then the door. I am still hearing radios and TV's only now they are sounding like they are right beside me. That's how clean I can hear them. Usually the voices, etc. sounded like they were in a distance. I don't feel like I've had a lot of stress on me lately so I don't understand why I am not able to sleep like I used to or why all of sudden I am being bombarded with voices all around me.

One time (in my minds eye), I was on my ceiling looking down on my bed and I could see myself as well as a smaller thing beside me. As this smaller thing moved closer to me, I would move away. Finally, I ran out of bed to move in and that was when I felt something touch my leg. I jumped out of my bed and put my back up against the wall. I was looking at my bed and was telling myself that there was nothing in my bed. I kept trying to tell myself, logically, that there was nothing there. However, I still had to pull back my sheets to reassure my eyes. I was frightened. I actually felt something touch me and it freaked me out.

Another time I saw a silhouette of a woman standing in my bedroom doorway. Although I couldn't see her face, I could tell she was dressed up very fancy. However, not a dress anyone would wear in this era. When I got out of bed to go see her I lost sight of her because of the angle of my bed to the doorway. Of course, when I got there, she was gone.

I have also been having rage lately. I am trying so hard to hide it from my family, but it's causing more internal turmoil. Ian has noticed that something has changed in me. He can tell by the look on my face (or rather the lack of look on my face). Apparently, I am talking in my sleep again. He said it sounded like I was very angry. It also looks like I'm fighting in my sleep.

Something else had changed too. I am getting terrible headaches now. They come on so fast. It is as If I have been hit in the head with a hammer. I hardly ever get headaches so these headaches worry me. I don't want to go back to the hospital, but I don't want to hurt my family again. I am very confused right now.

After I saw my Doctor on Feb. 7th, 2005, I went to the pharmacist to get my refills. I had enough medication to do me until Feb. 10th. On Friday the 11th, I opened the bag that had my refills in it and started to put them in my pill container. I didn't notice until the next day that I didn't have enough Effexor. I thought nothing of it because I knew I was going to see my Doctor on the 21st and I could do without the Effexor until then. By Saturday afternoon, I started to feel funny but didn't relate it to the lack of Effexor. Saturday night I tried to reach for the remote and ended up putting my hand in my cup of tea, spilling it on my chair. I felt agitated about that but still had not related it to the lack of my drug. On Sunday, I had slept to 1:00pm. I remember telling Ian coming into the bedroom and asking if I was going to get up at all. I told him yes because we had errands to run. I promptly fell back to sleep. We were also going to my Mother-in-Laws birthday dinner. Everything seemed OK except for the waves of dizziness I had been getting since Friday before. That night when we got home, Ian had made me a cup of coffee. The same as the night before, I went to reach for something and spilled my coffee all over me. I then felt intense rage and agitation. When the Doctor's office opened on Monday, I called and left a message for the Doctor to call the pharmacist and refill my Effexor. I had every confidence that I would get the prescription because there was approximately 7 hours before the pharmacist closed. As my day progressed, my mood was getting worse. I knew that if I didn't get the prescription right away I felt I would have to go to the hospital before I had a complete meltdown.

Holly got home from school that day and immediately knew something was wrong. I looked like I had been crying all day. I told her I had been and that I felt that I could possibly end up in my hospital that night. Well that set her off in a rampage. She was determined to get me my medication no matter what. I told her not to do anything just yet because I had until 7:00pm before the Doctor left for the day.

It was now getting close to 7:00 and she just couldn't wait anymore. She went to the pharmacist and asked if a refill had been called down from the Doctor's office for me. When he told her no, she went to the Doctor's office and demanded to see the Doctor. She got the prescription for me. My Doctor called me at home and asked me what was happening. I told him that I felt like I was drowning. What I meant was that I was sinking further and further into the depth of despair and I couldn't get out of it.

When Ian called me that night I couldn't even speak so I handed the phone to my daughter. She explained everything to him but told him not to worry because she was going to stay with me. If I did have to go to the hospital, her girlfriend would take me. She kept Ian updated throughout the night. The next day Ian couldn't believe the change in my. He said it was like night and day.

For a while now I have been seeing black Images (like shadows) run past my downstairs window. All

I see are pant legs and it feels to me like it is a male. The first time this happened, I went outside to check but there was no one there. When it happened again (only a few hours later) I ignored it. The black Images I see in my house are like black dots and again they go by so fast I only just catch them out of the corner of my eyes. Once I was in the kitchen, I saw a woman go by my front window, and she was dressed in white. Similar to the woman I saw standing in my bedroom doorway. She didn't move as fast as the black shadows but she still went by quickly. I went out my front door to see if there were any footsteps in my garden and of course, there were none. My garden is right at my front window so I would know if someone had been out there.

I am still hearing radios and TV's. I am also continuing to hear other people talking around me (not to me) although I cannot make out what they are saying. It is just a group of people all talking at once and I feel like I am on the outside looking in.

The newest and strangest thing that is happening to me is in my pillow. When I lay on my right side I can hear talking, music, etc. through my pillow as If I had speakers there. There was one time when a large dog barked from my pillow. I remember lifting my head and looking at my pillow. I couldn't help but laugh at this one. I have never owned a dog so it is not as If I have a dead dog trying to reach out to me.

Ian also informed me that I am back to kicking around at night. He said I yawn and snore at the same time (If that's possible). However, with me you never know. He said that after about 3 or 4 hours I seem to calm down.

August 12, 2005 - This is my first day of meditation. I figured if I started meditation, it would calm me down and keep me relaxed.

August 13, 2005 – Trust in your Angels, and believe in God.

This day when I meditated I saw a pure clear crystal (like a prism).

August 14, 2005 – This third day of meditation I was walking up a dark path through a forest. The trees were so high they blocked out the sun. I was holding hands with a two-year-old boy and we were both happy. I could actually feel what the boy felt. I was not at all afraid of the darkness. Suddenly we were at the edge of the forest and when I stepped out of the forest, I felt the intense heat of the sun. It felt great. I closed my eyes and put my face up toward the sun. Feeling the sun on my face and a slight breeze in the air made me feel total elation. My heart felt so happy it is hard to explain. I looked back to where I had just come from and the boy was gone. The only thought that came to my mind then was "yeah though I walk through the valley of the shadow of death, I shall fear no evil for though art with me..."

August 19, 2005 – Not all my meditations have shown me things, but I do get the most peaceful and relaxing sleep.

It has been a while but I am hearing telephones ring. In addition, the voices I now hear are in front of me as if I am talking face to face with someone. I still see the little black dots but I don't turn my head to see them anymore.

For some reason, on August 30th and 31st, I felt like crying. Just unexpectedly I go to speak and tears well up in my eyes. I went to see a Medium with a sister not too long ago. As soon as I walked into the door, he said, "Who is Ivy"? I said I was. He said I am going to read you first because when I meditated all I saw for you was stress, stress, stress. He told me there was a lot of stress around me and that if I didn't stop trying to help so many people I will crash. He told me I needed to take time out for myself in order to heal.

September 28, 2005 – I had a vision of the right side of a roof from either a large house or a barn. I think it is a house.

October 2, 2005 – Yes it is definitely a house. This time I aw it from the front. It is set up high on a hill so I could only see the top windows. I couldn't seem to move any closer to the house than the front of the driveway. I can't even set foot on the driveway. When I looked behind me, I could see the path that led to the house. This is the same path that the child had just lead me out of.

I also had a quick vision of a junior league's locker room. These were just small children because the lockers were low to the ground. Nothing hung in these lockers, but in the middle of the room was a long wooden bench. All the equipment was on this bench. It seemed like it was the end of a hockey season for this team. The team colours were black and silver, although I could not make out the logo. I called my sister because she had two sons in hockey. She said both of their uniforms were black and gold not black and silver.

I have stopped putting dates on my visions because I write them down days after I have had these visions. I had a vision of these wings but in the middle was a void. I couldn't see if it was a male or female figure. As the wings expanded, I could see just how huge they were. They were very thick at the part that came out from between the shoulders. All of this was black and the area surrounding it was a soft gray. It was almost as if I was seeing it as a negative. I was completely awestruck by the size of these wings.

I had been asking my main guardian angel what his or her name is. Finally, after about two weeks of asking, the name Edward flashed in my mind. Whether or not that is his name, that is now what I call him.

I had asked Edward to help me see with my third eye. You see, I have been accused of stealing a lap top computer and this accusation greatly disturbed me. I have never ever been accused of stealing anything in my life. I asked Edward to show me a sign that I was being watched over and protected. What I got was the right eye only of about 4 or 5 eyes. I'm taking that as a sign from Edward that I have 4 or 5 guardians watching over me. Thank you Edward.

Today I saw my Dad's wedding band going slowly around in circles. It was as if it was on an invisible ring hold in a display window. It was just going around by itself. The background was pure black.

Chapter 15
Conclusion

I have given you a tiny glimpse into my life. There are far too many things that have happened in my life to write them all down.

While writing this book, I suspect that I have always been bi-polar. It took 43 years for me to hit the "brick wall". This may seem odd but I am glad it happened to me. Now I understand my life. Even though I still have episodes, at least now I can handle them with the love, support, and understanding of my family

*Bi-Polar disorder is a recurrent disorder. It typically consists of three states:

1. A high state, called "mania
2. A low state, called "depression"
3. A well state, during which many people feel normal and function well.

As the person ages, the episodes of illness come closer together.

Mania and My Symptoms: Sometimes, a person may seem abnormally and continuously high, irritable or expansive for at least one week. If this change in mood is accompanied by other symptoms, the person may be in a manic phase of the bi-polar illness. Not everybody who enters a manic phase feels happy or euphoric. Instead, a person may feel very irritable, or may be terribly angry, disruptive, and aggressive. People in a manic phase do not just have mood symptoms. They have at least three other symptoms to an important degree. In my case, it is the ones listed below.

1. Less need for sleep – People feel rested after just a few hours of sleep. Sometimes they may not sleep at all for a few days or even weeks.
2. Flight of ideas or racing thoughts – People easily lost their train of thought, and have trouble interacting because they are easily distracted. They may be impatient with others who cannot follow their fast thinking and changing plans or ideas.
3. Worthlessness and Guilt – When depressed, individuals may lack self-confidence. They may not assert themselves, and they may be overwhelmed by feelings of worthlessness. Many people cannot stop thinking about past events.
4. Psychotic Symptoms – They may also hear (auditory hallucinations) or may see things that do not exist (visual hallucinations).

"Co morbidity" and its Importance – A "co morbid disorder" is an illness or medical condition that occurs together with another illness or medical condition. Co morbid conditions can occur with bi-polar disorder – they can start either before a bi-polar illness or at the same time.

Other Psychiatric conditions that often co-occur with bi-polar disorder:

Panic disorder

Obsessive-compulsive disorder

It is important to diagnose co morbidity in bi-polar disorder. Co morbid conditions may cloud the clinical picture and complicate treatment of bi-polar disorder. In addition, the co morbid conditions are often so severe they too need treating. However, in my case, the medication I am on for bi-polar has controlled my panic disorder and my compulsive behaviors. Now that I think about it, I do not think I even told my Doctor I had OCB, but he will know now.

What is a "trigger" for a bi-polar episode? – Feeling very stressed or continually losing sleep is an example of this kind of trigger.

Getting Treatment for your family member – Most jurisdictions in North American have mental health laws that make it hard to hospitalize people against their will. People can only be forced into hospital if they threaten to harm themselves or other, or if they cannot care for themselves. For me it was the threat to harm myself or others.

Remember, when people threaten suicide, they are usually pleading for help. They should be taken seriously. Suicidal thinking is most often a temporary emotional state. During this phase, a person needs to be kept safe. Similarly, manic episodes can make a person behave dangerously with serious consequences. In my case, it was my erratic driving. Manic patients are therefore best treated in hospital.

*The above information is available in full at www.camh.net. I highly recommend that this web site be looked at before jumping to any conclusions about an illness of a loved one.

I am now at the point in my life where I am in charge again. People depend on me. I am organized. I feel free, as if a weight has been lifted off my shoulders.

I have never hidden the fact that I am Bi-Polar. My family, friends, co-workers, etc. all know that I have a mental illness. I can go for months at a time without crashing and because of this, people tend to forget I am Bi-Polar. It is only when I crash that they remember.

Since being diagnosed as Bi-Polar my attitude has changed towards many things in my life. I make people laugh because of my quirkiness and wit. I have had several people tell me that they haven't had a good laugh in a long time that it actually makes them feel good to laugh again. I see things differently as well. I no longer want to die. I want to watch my children grow up. I want to be with my husband (best friend). I miss my family if they are away from me for even one day.

When I was diagnosed, my family had consultations with our family Doctor to help them cope with what has happened to me. Our Doctor told them that they could mimic my symptoms because they themselves are confused and upset with the sudden change in me.

As the years have gone by, we have all settled into our familiar routines again. This has made us closer than ever before.

This is the reason why I wrote this book. Instead of only clinical terms being used, I have tried to have you understand the diagnosis of depression and bi-polar in laymen's terms. Please watch out for the symptoms. This may not be easy, especially if symptoms start in early adolescents. Another problem that makes it harder is the fact that the manic episodes can be explained away as something else. If someone seems to be in a bad mood, we just simply say this person is having a bad day and dismiss it at that.

As in my case, symptoms were showing up when I was twelve. It started with feeling of worthlessness and continued with anger, rage, self-loathing, self-harming, suicidal thoughts, as well as other symptoms.

When I hit the "brick wall" that was the beginning of a diagnosis of depression, hospitalization and finally diagnosis of bi-polar.

If you start noticing unusual symptoms with a friend or family member try writing it down. You may feel like you are spying on the person or that the person is having an especially happy or bad day. However, if you write them down you may, over time, be able to notice a pattern that something is not quite right. You may want to discuss what you have noticed with other family members to see if they have noticed changes in this person. I do not suggest confronting the person and telling him/her what you have notices because the person may not want to hear it because of denial or that you are too nosey. Also, do not have the friends/family members' gang up on the person as this may cause the person to feel spied on. Do your homework and solid research, and then discuss this with your Doctor. The Doctor will confirm or deny your suspicions and what the next step should be.

Concurrent disorders (CD for short) generally describes a situation in which a person experiences psychiatric disorder and/or a gambling disorder for example. My other disorder was compulsion. I would become compulsive with something until I got bored with what I was doing. However, my compulsions would last anywhere from six months to years. The fact that both of my husbands indulged me in my compulsions only compounded my problem. It was not until after I was put on medication for bi-polar that I realized I even had OCD. That is a whole new other book to write. Now I am content to stay at home. I am sure, after my Doctor reads this book; he is going to want to have a good talk with me about some of the things I have revealed in the book that I have not spoken to him about.

On a personal note, I wonder if we are not just living with bi-polar, but in fact are also reliving some past life experiences as well. Maybe we do not have a mental Illness but rather a mental ability and are unaware or do not believe in these abilities.

It was not until I was re-reading my manuscript that made me aware of pieces of my life now that were intertwined with past lives.

Are we re-living snippets of out other lives in parallel to this one? I think that only psychiatrists should do a test on their patients having them write down as much information about their lives as they can recall. Whether it be an odd or recurring dream, strange thoughts, visions they do not understand, voices they hear, etc. Have the patient delve into their childhood as well. Did they have invisible friends that they talked to or played with as children?

Get as much information as possible in writing from childhood to the present day. Once the test is done, read what your patient has written. Make sure to read everything with an open mind and do not judge or disclude anything because of your own beliefs.

It could be that the sub-conscious mind is giving the conscious mind information about past lives. With this information coming to light in this life from a past life could be the reason why people with bi-polar cannot express their thoughts in a stable way. This may make professionals think these people are mentally unstable. Hence the label of bi-polar disorder.

If they had childhood friends that no one else could see could in fact be their guardian angels. As we grow up, we dismiss or completely forget that there were invisible friends. I know that parents would dismiss this as a childish behavior.

Could it also be that bi-polar's have some sort of psychic ability they are not aware of? A mixture of pieces of past lives with a bit of psychic ability would also make the patient seem even more unstable than others.

These thoughts would never have occurred to me if I had not written this book. Reading and re-reading my manuscript has opened my eyes to the above possibilities.

After testing the patients and sorting out their thoughts, have the patients hypnotized. Take them to the most recent past life and record this session. There may be a strong link not recognized before.

Even If I am entirely wrong about this, at the very least, you will have more information about your patients that you may not have known before. In either case, you may understand your patients more and may be able to adjust medications accordingly.

I have always had a fear of falling down stairs. With the knowledge of having seen myself fall down stairs to my death, I now understand why that particular fear exists in me today. Now that I am aware of it being a part of a past life, I can dismiss this fear in this life.

About The Author

Author Ivy Berry and her Husband Ian.

My name is Ivy-Leanne Berry. I was born in Etobicoke, Ontario, Canada on Sunday, March 13, 1960.

I am now 47 years old and writing my first book. I don't know what has possessed me to write this book, but here it is.

I have so many thoughts racing through my mind that I have to put it in writing.

I hope you enjoyed this book and hopefully it will touch someone's life in a positive way. I also hope it helps a family or family member's to understand the diagnosis of Bi-polar (also known as Manic Depression).